The Prayer Jar

DEVOTIONAL

HEALING

The Prayer Jar

DEVOTIONAL

HEALING

WANDA E. BRUNSTETTER

with

JANICE THOMPSON

BARBOUR
PUBLISHING

Print ISBN 978-1-63609-929-3

Member of the
Evangelical Christian
Publishers Association

Printed in China.

HEALING

To "heal" means to make well again, or to cure or make whole to a sound healthy condition. This can apply to physical, emotional, or spiritual illness. Healing emotionally or spiritually can often be more difficult than healing physically. Some people hold grudges and become bitter about things that have been said or done to them in the past. They let it affect their relationships, and their spiritual life suffers as well. Hurts from things that have happened to us often go deep and can leave a scar or open wound if not dealt with properly and given the opportunity to heal.

When things don't go as we planned or people let us down, it's easy to become bitter and unforgiving. We sometimes feel disappointed with God. The truth is, though, we can always rely on Him. He's forever faithful in all that He does. We can go to God when things go wrong. He is our refuge and help. Our heavenly Father is the God of healing. God is aware of our thoughts and actions. He knows our emotional and spiritual pain that needs to be healed. There's hope for the chains of our past wounds to be broken.

My hope is that this devotional book will help everyone who reads it to fully understand the importance of the true meaning of physical, emotional, and spiritual healing. When we reach out to God in prayer and are willing to share the burdens on our hearts, healing begins.

HEALING HEARTS:
EMOTIONAL SCARS

A physical scar from an injury is often visible on the outside, but an emotional scar cannot be seen.

Difficult experiences from past relationships can create emotional scars that must be dealt with to heal and develop empathy for others. Sometimes an emotional scar is created by a single traumatic event, but often dozens of smaller scars are from events we may not remember and are deeply rooted in our unconscious mind.

There's no quick fix for healing emotional scars. It takes time and effort, but with God's help, it can be done. The act of looking inward at our emotional pain can feel traumatic and cause us to avoid talking or even thinking about it. However, one of the most important aspects of healing emotionally is to talk to someone you trust—a close friend, relative, or counselor. Prayer and meditation on God's Word are beneficial for emotional healing. Exercising and journaling can help with depression and put our thoughts into perspective. Even so, an emotional wound can never truly heal without forgiveness. Unforgiveness and bitterness are like an infection. Once you've forgiven and worked through your pain, your life can be a testimony to others, and your heart will be filled with peace. Jesus promised in John 14:27 (NKJV), "Peace I leave with you, My peace I give to you; not as the world gives do I give to you. Let not your heart be troubled, neither let it be afraid."

A BINDER OF WOUNDS

He heals the brokenhearted and binds up their wounds.

PSALM 147:3 NIV

Picture Jesus, Savior of the world, bending down to heal a blind man. A beggar. An outcast. The Creator of all bent low to care for the needs of one whom others would walk by.

The pain of rejection, grief, and confusion must surely have consumed this man, who never expected a visitation from the King of kings on that ordinary day. But isn't it just like Jesus to sweep in when least expected and bring healing to broken bodies, broken hearts, and broken lives?

No matter how long you've felt invisible, you are seen by the Savior of the world today. He bears witness to the brokenness, the heartache, and the confusion. In the middle of it all, He stops and looks you in the eye, with grace flooding the space between you.

And then, in that miraculous way of His, He bends low and touches you, driving out the brokenness. Your heart is mended and your thoughts transformed.

What a good, good Savior, who heals the broken!

Thank You, Jesus, for bending low and for
touching me in my brokenness. Amen.

PRAYER JAR INSPIRATION:

From heaven to earth, Lord, You bring
healing to all who call out to You!

HE'S EVER CLOSE

*The Lord is close to the brokenhearted and
saves those who are crushed in spirit.*

PSALM 34:18 NIV

Have you ever walked through a valley so deep that you couldn't see beyond it? Oftentimes those gut-wrenching experiences cause us to withdraw from society, to pull away from family and friends, and to slip into isolation.

It's hard to stay connected when we're hurting, but it's vital. God created us to live in community. But here's a solid truth: even when you're physically alone, you're never truly alone. God is always with you, even in the deepest valley. He's ever close to the brokenhearted and saves those who are crushed in spirit. No matter how deep, no matter how complex, He's right there, as near as your next cry for help.

If you need healing for the emotional scars and psychological wounds you've endured, look up! Jesus is standing nearby with healing in His wings!

*Thank You for sticking close, Jesus.
Even when others leave me, You never will.*

PRAYER JAR INSPIRATION:

The heavenly Father is as close as your next heartbeat.

A NEW LINEAGE

By faith the prostitute Rahab, because she welcomed the spies, was not killed with those who were disobedient.

HEBREWS 11:31 NIV

Have you ever read the story of Rahab? She's listed in the book of Joshua as a harlot, so (based solely on that description) you wouldn't think the Bible had much good to say about her. But Rahab's story changed dramatically when she allowed herself to be used of God to protect the Jewish people.

Rahab became the mother of Boaz. And, if you know the remarkable story of Ruth, you know that she ended up married to Boaz, her kinsman redeemer.

Rahab, who was known only to her neighbors and passers-by as "the harlot," is one of the few women listed in the lineage of Jesus.

When your story changes, when you allow God to bring healing and wholeness, everything changes. A new plot is written. The old tale is no more. (Bring on the new writers! This story's getting a facelift!)

Thank You for rewriting my story, Lord! I'm so glad You've given me a brand-new lineage! Amen.

PRAYER JAR INSPIRATION:

Plot twist! Jesus has changed my story!

RESTORED!

" 'But I will restore you to health and heal your
wounds,' declares the LORD, 'because you are called
an outcast, Zion for whom no one cares.' "
JEREMIAH 30:17 NIV

Have you ever thought about how God created the human body to heal itself? Scrape your knee and a scab forms. Over time, healing comes to the area. The body works to mend the broken place. It just takes time.

Sometimes mental, emotional, and spiritual healing take time too. God covers the wound, insulating it, much like a scab. Then, over time, you're able to begin to function properly again. The pain diminishes.

Don't get dismayed if your healing is taking time. Don't get angry at yourself if those old feelings crop up again. Just do your best to give them to God and trust the healing process.

He will restore you. That's a promise. He will heal those emotional and psychological wounds because He loves you and wants you to be set free. Trust the God of the process.

You're healing me even now, Lord!
I'm grateful, no matter how long it takes.

PRAYER JAR INSPIRATION:

My healing will be worth the wait.

11

PRAISE AHEAD
OF THE HEALING

*Heal me, LORD, and I will be healed; save me and I
will be saved, for you are the one I praise.*
JEREMIAH 17:14 NIV

Part of the healing process is learning to praise even before your healing
comes. It doesn't make sense in the natural world, but turning your
eyes on Jesus—singing His praises and trusting in His promises—
causes you to look away from your own problems and focus on Him.

Something amazing happens when you lift your eyes off your
pain or your problem and place them squarely on Jesus. Suddenly
you have a completely different perspective. Trust increases. Hope
increases. Faith rises.

So praise Jesus today! He's worthy of your praise whether you've
seen complete healing yet or not. Praise Him, not just as a distraction from any pain you might be facing, but as a simple act of love
and obedience to a Savior who gave His very life for you. That's how
much He loves you!

*Today I offer praise to You, my Savior, even before full healing
comes. You are worthy, no matter what I'm walking through.*

PRAYER JAR INSPIRATION:

Even when I'm in the valley, my God is still worthy of praise.

HE'S NOT FROWNING!

*The sacrifices of God are a broken spirit; a broken and
a contrite heart, God, You will not despise.*

PSALM 51:17 NASB

Aren't you glad God doesn't frown down on you when you have the blues? It would be awful to think that your sadness was somehow upsetting Him. Of course He wants you to put your trust in Him, but if anyone understands a broken heart, God does! He gave His only Son, after all. How heartbreaking must it have been to watch His only child die for a crime He did not commit—and all out of love for mankind.

Yes, your heavenly Father certainly understands your broken and contrite heart. He knows what to heal, when to heal, and how to heal. And you can trust Him with every single step of that process, even when it feels like the pain will never end.

Today, give God your broken heart. Picture it in His capable hands, being gently wooed back to hope and joy. Only the God of the universe is capable of such a miracle. But He loves you enough to perform it on your behalf.

*Lord, I place my heart in Your capable hands!
I know I can trust You! Amen.*

PRAYER JAR INSPIRATION:

My God isn't frowning down on me—not today, not ever.

13

TRANSFORMED BY JOY

A joyful heart is good medicine, but a broken spirit dries up the bones.
PROVERBS 17:22 NASB

What a wonder joy is! It transforms everything. When you add joy to the recipe, the outcome is always good. It's like ointment to an open wound. When you apply it liberally—even in the darkest moment—it works 100 percent of the time. And best of all, it's a gift that comes along with salvation.

Joy energizes. Joy lifts. Joy engages you with the giver. Joy casts your vision off of yourself and onto Him. Is it any wonder we sing "Joy to the World!" at Christmastime? That is our ultimate wish for every heart, every nation, to experience the fullness of joy that Christ brings, the blissful message of hope!

Whatever you're walking through today, apply the joy of your salvation, and then watch your circumstances change. Healing comes on the wings of a celebration, the kind that begins to praise even before answers come. (What are you waiting for? Start praising!)

I'll start celebrating now, Lord, because my
joyful heart will give me hope! Amen.

PRAYER JAR INSPIRATION:

I can be transformed by joy.

A THOUSAND TIMES BETTER

This will bring health to your body and nourishment to your bones.

PROVERBS 3:8 NIV

We've all had those emails or text messages from well-meaning friends trying to sell us their latest and greatest supplements or weight-loss plans. Those would-be salespeople are quite exuberant in their presentation—in part because they've seen results in their own bodies. (Hey, when you find something that works, you like to tell others so they can experience it too!)

The Word of God is like those supplements, only a thousand times better. The words you find inside the pages of the Bible really will bring life to your body and nourishment to your bones. They are a healing balm, better than anything you could ever swallow in pill form.

And no matter what you're walking through, there's a biblical remedy, easily found in the Word of God. Heartache? There are verses for you. Physical pain? You'll find verses for that too.

Talk about a miracle cure! The healing capabilities of the Word are endless! (And *bonus*: no multilevel marketing schemes involved!)

I will turn to You and Your Word, Lord. I put my trust
in You to heal the broken places in my heart.

PRAYER JAR INSPIRATION:

Thank You for the best supplement of all, Jesus—Your Word!

AN END DATE

The human spirit can endure in sickness, but
a crushed spirit who can bear?
Proverbs 18:14 niv

Having a cold is nothing to sneeze at. Illnesses like that can be downright debilitating, taking you away from your family and your work for days on end. But even in the worst of it, you hang on to one important fact: you will get better. You might need medicine. You need rest. But the common cold passes in time. And knowing your negative situation has an end date helps so much psychologically.

Now think about those who are heartsick. They can't see an end date. They're in the thick of it, thinking the pain will go on forever. That's why it's so critical to give hope to the hopeless—so they can see a way out.

No matter how difficult the situation, no matter how bruised your heart, there is an end date to your pain. Focus on Jesus, the author and finisher of your faith. Remember how much He loves you. And remind yourself, "This too shall pass." It will, you know. But you must give it to Him first.

Today I make a visible demonstration of giving You my pain, Jesus.
I'm ready to see the end date and to walk in hope once again!

PRAYER JAR INSPIRATION:

This intense pain has an end date. When I give a difficult situation
to Jesus, I can live in hope, knowing it will pass in time.

BEAUTIFUL SCARS

Make me hear joy and gladness, that the bones
You have broken may rejoice.

PSALM 51:8 NKJV

Some scars are visible on the outside. They're difficult to mask. When you meet a person who has been burned in a fire, for instance, they share their scars as a testimony to what they've survived.

Other scars are buried deep, not visible to the outside world. Oh, you know they're there. You've survived a lot in your life, and those scars are a badge of honor. But sometimes you wonder if they're getting in the way.

Here's the truth: scars are the body's way of healing. They're an outward sign that internal healing has taken place. And when the heart is involved, internal scars form. But those scars are tough! They're working like glue to bind things together. And they're a clear sign of what has been, not of what is or what is coming.

So, embrace those scars. As the psalm says, rejoice—scars and all. Wear them proudly as a sign of victory. God has done an amazing work in your life!

I'm grateful for the scars, Lord. They're a
reminder of all You've brought me through.

PRAYER JAR INSPIRATION:

My scars are beautiful because they announce, "Healing has come!"

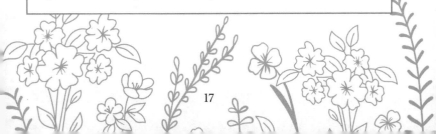

PLENTY OF LIFE AHEAD

*Have mercy on me, Lord, for I am faint; heal
me, Lord, for my bones are in agony.*

PSALM 6:2 NIV

If you're getting up there in years, the "bones are in agony" part of today's verse might hit a little too close to home. As we age, sometimes our bones seem to cry out in agony when we stand after sitting for a long period of time. It's as if we must wake them up and coax them into submission!

After a bit of stretching and flexing, we're finally able to make it from the sofa to the kitchen to start dinner. And once we get loosened up, we're good to go.

That's what it's like after you've been through an emotionally scarring time. Those scars can tighten things up. You're not as emotionally nimble as you once were. But you can learn to use those scars to your advantage. The key is to get up. Get going. Don't allow yourself to remain stagnant in one spot. True healing comes as you start moving. (Moving is an act of faith for the one locked up in pain.)

Up, friend! Off the sofa you go. There's plenty of life ahead once you get moving.

*I need Your help to start moving in faith, Lord!
Loosen up these emotional joints, and let's get going! Amen.*

PRAYER JAR INSPIRATION:

With God's help, I can move even when I don't feel like it.

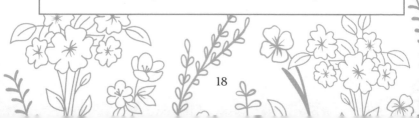

OH, THOSE EMOTIONS!

So I say, walk by the Spirit, and you will not gratify the desires of the flesh. For the flesh desires what is contrary to the Spirit, and the Spirit what is contrary to the flesh. They are in conflict with each other, so that you are not to do whatever you want.

GALATIANS 5:16–17 NIV

Emotions are fickle things. They change with the wind. Maybe you've been there—up one minute, down the next. Excited about life, then plummeting to the depths of despair.

Emotions are a bit like the tail on a kite. They flutter around uncontrollably in the rear. Emotions often show up after the real issue hits you. Tears come when you're grieving. A broken heart brings you to your knees after your spouse leaves you. Joy rises in your soul after you get great news.

Emotions come after. But you know what comes before, during, *and* after? The God of creation. He's there before the crisis. He's there in the center of it. And He's there to bring healing and comfort after the fact.

Don't be too hard on yourself if you're emotional. But remember that God created you and knows you better than anyone—even your emotional side. And He's right there to bring healing when you need it.

I'm so glad you see past my emotions, Lord!
You created me and know me best of all.

PRAYER JAR INSPIRATION:

I won't let my emotions rule me.

HIS CAPABLE HANDS

*My sacrifice, O God, is a broken spirit; a broken and
contrite heart you, God, will not despise.*

PSALM 51:17 NIV

If you could see a broken heart with your eyes, what would it look like?
Do you envision a heart-shaped object with cracks running through it?

When you're in an emotionally challenging season, you might
feel like it's never ending. When a loved one dies. When a spouse
leaves. When your best friend betrays you. When you lose your job.
These kinds of things are a kick to the gut. And the pain is real. It's
deep. It's relentless.

Picture that broken heart, the one with all the cracks, being picked
up by your heavenly Father. He takes it into His very capable hands
and, with just a whisper, every crack is filled. Love glues it all back
together. Somehow that fragile heart is now capable of holding more
than pain.

Joy returns. Hope returns. Peace returns. And all because you were
willing to give your heart to Him. So, what's holding you back? Place
it in His capable hands today.

*Take my brokenness and make me whole, Jesus!
In Your hands, my heart can be mended. Amen.*

PRAYER JAR INSPIRATION:

Jesus mends every crack in my broken heart.

THE THINGS YOU CAN'T CONTROL

A time to weep and a time to laugh,
a time to mourn and a time to dance.

ECCLESIASTES 3:4 NIV

There are so many things in life you simply can't control. Many of the circumstances that swirl around you are unchangeable. You can't fix them.

That's why it's important to control the things you can. Behaviors. Attitudes. Forgiveness. Discipline. Taking charge of the areas of your life that are controllable honors God.

No matter what's swirling outside your door at the moment, pause and do business with the Lord over the things you have control over. Give Him your heart. Your thoughts. Your attitude. Your past. Your present. Your future.

You do your part. He does His part. Together you're an amazing team. And remember, this is only a season. This situation won't last forever.

Thank You for guiding me through this tough season, Jesus! Amen.

PRAYER JAR INSPIRATION:

Jesus is on my team!

FIXING WHAT
YOU CAN'T SEE

That is what the Scriptures mean when they say, "No eye has seen, no ear has heard, and no mind has imagined what God has prepared for those who love him."

1 Corinthians 2:9 NLT

How can you fix something you can't see with your own eyes or hear with your own ears? Emotions aren't visible or audible (unless there's sobbing or laughter involved). They're illusive, invisible things. And yet they're very real.

So how do you go about fixing what you cannot see?

You put your trust in God. He sees. He hears. He knows. To Him, your emotions are completely visible. And He already has a plan to take you beyond where you are to a land of plenty, a place where broken things will all be mended.

While you're waiting and while you're trying to figure out why the pain is still so fresh, do your best to place your trust in God and to imagine a time (it's coming!) when things will be better.

They will, you know.

I put my trust in You, Lord. You see all things. You know all things. And You love me even more than I love myself! Amen.

PRAYER JAR INSPIRATION:

I can't see, but Jesus can.

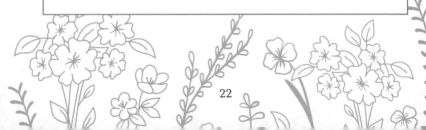

A LENGTHY LIST

Keep your heart with all vigilance,
for from it flow the springs of life.
PROVERBS 4:23 ESV

If someone asked you to write down all the emotions, what would your list look like? No doubt you would include joy, anger, sorrow, grief, and so on.

If you do a deep dive into emotions, you'll learn that there are (categorically) six of them: happiness, sadness, fear, disgust, anger, and surprise. Some of the things we deal with (like frustration, for instance) might fall under the category of disgust or anger.

Now think about emotional healing. If you experience brokenness in any one of these six categories, imagine how it would affect the others. If sadness consumes you, it wipes away happiness. If you're overwhelmed by disgust at something a spouse has done, it triggers anger. They all play together (or squabble together) in the same play yard.

Now you see why it's so important to allow God to fully heal every area of your heart. One area usually overlaps another. So allow Him to do a deep dive into all six areas so that total healing can come.

I give all my emotions to You, Jesus, not just a few!

PRAYER JAR INSPIRATION:

Jesus sees every emotion and knows how to bring healing.

CALL IT OUT!

*Dear friend, I pray that you may enjoy good health and that all
may go well with you, even as your soul is getting along well.*

3 JOHN 1:2 NIV

Imagine you had an open wound in a hidden place where no one could
see it. You did your best to treat it, but without proper antibiotics the
infection continued to spread. You would probably do your best to
hide the problem from others to make sure they didn't see the extent
of the infection. But before long, that would prove difficult. No doubt
you would have to change the way you walked. The way you sat. Your
level of focus doing ordinary things would change.

A hidden wound affects everything. And if left untended, it can
become septic. At that point, there's no hiding the problem anymore.
Your very life is in danger.

This might seem like an extreme example, but when you refuse to
acknowledge the problems going on in your broken heart, they will
eventually catch up with you. There will be no hiding the problem
once you reach the septic point.

So don't wait. Run to Jesus today. Allow the spiritual antibiotic
of His love, His peace, His joy to wash over the wound so that true
healing can come.

I've waited long enough, Lord. Today is my day for healing to begin!

PRAYER JAR INSPIRATION:

Why wait for healing when God can begin the work today?

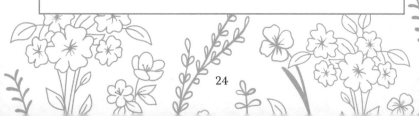

A SKIPPING HEART

*The LORD is my strength and my shield; my heart
trusts in him, and he helps me. My heart leaps
for joy, and with my song I praise him.*

PSALM 28:7 NIV

Have you ever known someone who had to have a defibrillator installed? Perhaps this person struggled with an irregular heartbeat or even congestive heart failure, so the cardiologist recommended a defibrillator.

Simply put, a defibrillator restores a normal heartbeat by sending an electrical charge when necessary. It brings things back into alignment.

That's the same thing God longs to do in your emotional health. He wants to take that broken, skipping heart, the one that can't seem to control itself anymore, and restore its natural rhythm.

You can't do this on your own. (Ask any heart patient, and they will tell you they needed a medical intervention.)

You need an intervention too. And Jesus stands nearby, ready to offer just the right "charge" to bring your heart back into alignment. Trust Him. He knows your heart better than anyone else!

I will trust You to bring alignment in my heart and emotions, Jesus!

PRAYER JAR INSPIRATION:

God is the master physician, bringing all things into alignment!

FOR THE SAKE OF THE CHILDREN?

And the Word became flesh and dwelt among us,
and we have seen his glory, glory as of the only
Son from the Father, full of grace and truth.

JOHN 1:14 ESV

It's important for parents to heal, especially if they have children. After all, children are witnessing (and often mimicking) what they observe. But the kids aren't the only reason Mom and Dad need to get past the brokenness they're experiencing. They're God's kids too.

Let's face it: it's easy to say, "Get your act together for the sake of your children," but when we say that, we're overlooking the fact that Mom and Dad are as critical to God as those kids are. Yes, the children are vulnerable. And true, they're learning from their environment. But Jesus loves Mom and Dad too.

God wants everyone to be healed, not just so the kids can grow up in a healthy environment, but so that every single person in the household can experience the abundance of walking in healing and wholeness. *Every. Single. Person.*

Jesus didn't leave people out. When the woman with the issue of blood tugged on the hem of His garment, He didn't say, "I'm too busy to deal with you."

He's never too busy. He wants the whole family.

Today I offer myself and my whole family to You, Jesus!

PRAYER JAR INSPIRATION:

Healing—for Mom, Dad, and kids—that's God's heart for the family.

26

HEALING
PAST HURTS

Letting go of the past, including people who may have hurt you, involves accepting what you can't control, taking accountability, and focusing on the lessons learned. Seeking help is also important.

Sometimes, to heal, we need to *feel* it first. Bottling up our thoughts and emotions can hurt us more, making it hard to let go, especially if we dwell on the past and the things that harmed us.

Being accountable doesn't mean we have to blame ourselves for things that happened in the past. It's about realizing how much energy we spend on remembering the feelings we've had that are no longer in the present. It's also about choosing to focus our attention on something else. When we hold on to our hurtful memories, we're reliving the painful experience. This is likely to keep us stuck in the past, making it impossible to let go. You can choose where you put your mind and heart today. Not letting go of the past can cause you to miss the good things in your life right now.

Bible verses offer comfort, guidance, and hope when letting go of past hurts. They remind us that we're not alone in our struggles, and that God is with us, offering forgiveness, grace, and strength to move forward.

Jeremiah 29:11 (NKJV) says, "For I know the thoughts that I think toward you, says the LORD, thoughts of peace and not of evil, to give you a future and a hope."

FORGETTING
WHAT LIES BEHIND

*Of course, my friends, I really do not think that I have already won it;
the one thing I do, however, is to forget what is behind me and do my
best to reach what is ahead. So I run straight toward the goal in order to
win the prize, which is God's call through Christ Jesus to the life above.*

PHILIPPIANS 3:13–14 GNT

Forgetting the past sounds easy enough in theory. But sometimes letting go of yesterday isn't as simple as one might think.

If anyone understood this, Job did. In his rearview mirror, he saw a man with the perfect life: a home, a family, crops, cattle, friends, money. All the things a person could ever wish for.

Through the windshield, however, things looked a lot different. All those things he once cherished had been stripped away. And now came the hard task: deciding where to set his gaze. Looking back certainly wasn't going to fix anything. And if he looked too far ahead, he might get despondent.

Maybe you can relate. Maybe your rearview mirror reflects better days gone by and almost lost from memory. Or perhaps your yesterdays were so painful you don't want to risk even a glance.

No matter what you've been through—good or bad—God can help you focus on today. Right here, right now, He can give you the courage and strength to heal from the pain of your yesterdays.

*The only way I can truly forget what lies behind
me is to keep my gaze fixed on You, Jesus. Amen.*

PRAYER JAR INSPIRATION:

Yesterday is in the past. Today is a gift from God.

A CRUSHED SPIRIT

The human spirit can endure in sickness, but
a crushed spirit who can bear?
PROVERBS 18:14 NIV

Have you ever met someone who lived in the past? Maybe she buried herself in the memories of yesteryear. Or, perhaps (as many do) she camped out in the valley of past hurts.

Some people just can't seem to get past yesterday's wounds. They lick them. They baby them. They talk about them. They peel the scab off. . .on purpose. They draw attention to them. It's almost as if they enjoy the pain that yesterday's hurts caused.

But why? Why would someone live like that? Why adopt a "woe is me" mentality when it does nothing but drag you down? In part, because some people have made those past hurts their identity. They choose to identify as a wounded warrior, one with a crushed spirit.

God doesn't want you to place your identity in your battle wounds. He wants you to heal from them and move forward. So don't nurture those wounds. Don't rehearse them. Don't continue to publicize them. Instead, allow the King of kings to heal you from them once and for all.

Today I choose to allow healing of my past hurts, Jesus.
Completely. Totally. Heal me, I pray. Amen.

PRAYER JAR INSPIRATION:

I won't lick old wounds.

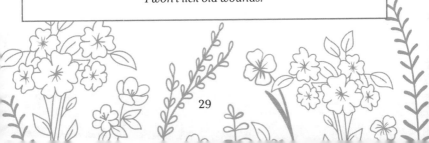

BINDER OF WOUNDS

He heals the brokenhearted and bandages their wounds.

PSALM 147:3 NLT

If you had a wound on your leg, would you allow it to fester, or would you open it and encourage the infection to come out? Neither option sounds very exciting, does it? But one leads to life and the other to death.

An oozing wound is nasty and painful, but if you don't get the infection out, the wound will only get worse. Opening it can seem arduous, but it's really the only way if you want to experience healing.

If you've been through a trauma in the past, you might still bear the scars of that today, in much the same way your leg would have a scar after that wound finally healed up. But isn't that better than doing nothing and allowing the infection to eventually overtake you?

God's ability to heal is remarkable—body, mind, and spirit! But you have a role to play to get that infection taken care of.

It's not always easy to open myself up to help,
but I need You, Lord. Heal me, I pray. Amen.

PRAYER JAR INSPIRATION:

God has the remarkable ability to heal all my wounds.

LIFE TO THE FULL!

"The thief comes only to steal and kill and destroy; I have
come that they may have life, and have it to the full."

JOHN 10:10 NIV

Sometimes we seek healing for the hurts in our past but hold on to behaviors that prevent us from living life to the full. Perhaps we go through a painful romantic breakup and manage to forgive the one who left, but we leave walls up. The next time someone comes along, we inadvertently push them away. These things happen.

It's important to pray for healing from hurts but also healing from behaviors that might bring us further harm. God wants the whole you healed—every little part. So, don't let anything remain behind. (Hey, when you clean a house, you don't leave a dirty bathroom or an icky stove!) Scrub those spots clean, and then move forward with confidence, guarded behaviors behind you. The same is true of your healing: get every single spot cleaned out so you can move forward in peace.

I truly want to leave the past in the past, Lord. If there's anything
left in me to be dealt with, I give it to You wholly and freely.

PRAYER JAR INSPIRATION:

God will sweep away every cobweb if I let Him.

TODAY

God again set a certain day, calling it "Today." This he did when a long time later he spoke through David, as in the passage already quoted: "Today, if you hear his voice, do not harden your hearts."

HEBREWS 4:7 NIV

When you read the word *yesterday*, what comes to mind? Did you realize the word only refers (specifically) to the day that came before today?

When we say "God wiped away the pain of all my yesterdays," we're talking about a lot of days, not just one. That's a lot of work on God's part! He took yesterday and did a work. He also took yesterday's yesterday and cleaned it up too. And so on.

He wants you to look beyond your yesterdays to the todays. Yesterday will give you a crick in your neck if you stare at it too long. Today is right in front of you, an empty page ready to be written on.

Just don't give God too much to have to deal with tomorrow, okay?

But even if you do, tomorrow's yesterday (today) is currently fresh and ready for amazing things to happen!

All my days are held in Your hands, Jesus.
I trust You with them all! Amen.

PRAYER JAR INSPIRATION:

I will redirect my attention—from yesterday to today!

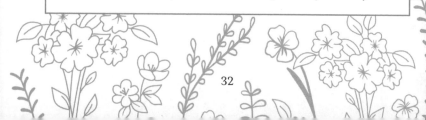

P.A.S.T.

See! The winter is past; the rains are over and gone.

SONG OF SONGS 2:11 NIV

What if you took the word *past* and broke it down into an acronym that looked like this:

P: Put
A: All
S: Situations
T: There (at the feet of Jesus)

What if you took all those situations from the past—the ones you couldn't control and even the ones you could (but messed up) and laid them at the feet of Jesus? How different would today look if you could stop fretting over yesterday?

When you lay something down, you remove your hands from it. It's not yours to fix anymore. And that's what the Bible encourages us to do with the things from the past anyway. There's no longer anything you can do with the stuff from days gone by. Even if you choose to pick it up, you can't change it. So put it there—at Jesus' feet.

Be relieved of the pressure. Be relieved of the guilt. Be relieved of the "what-ifs." Leave it in the PAST where it belongs, safe in the Savior's hands.

I don't know why I tend to pick things up after I've already laid them down, Jesus, but I want to stop. I'm going to need Your help. Amen.

PRAYER JAR INSPIRATION:

Today is tomorrow's yesterday.

DEFINE HURT

*And after you have suffered a little while, the God of all
grace, who has called you to his eternal glory in Christ,
will himself restore, confirm, strengthen, and establish you.*

1 Peter 5:10 esv

If you look up the definition of the word *hurt*, you'll see a lot of words
like *distress, physical damage* or *pain, injury, mental or emotional suffering,
hinder, impair, discomfort,* and *damage.*

There's not a positive word in the bunch. Not one.

When you're hurt, things can get complicated. There are varying
layers to the pain you've suffered. And they must be peeled back
like an onion, one layer after another. This takes time. And effort.
Sometimes, as the layers are exposed, even more pain is experienced,
which causes even more distress.

As the onion is being peeled, go easy on yourself. Grace is necessary,
and you can be the one both offering and receiving it at the same time.

Healing rarely happens all at once. But God will strengthen you.
You can count on it.

*Thank You for the promise of Your Word, Lord,
that You will restore and establish me. Amen.*

PRAYER JAR INSPIRATION:

When nothing seems positive, God's Word always is!

34

LINGERING

Let your eyes look straight ahead;
fix your gaze directly before you.
PROVERBS 4:25 NIV

Have you ever had a lingering cough or cold? What a nuisance, to have that icky hacking cough go on and on for days or even weeks. At some point you start thinking things like, *Am I going to have to live with this for the rest of my life?* It can feel like that in the moment.

That's kind of how it is when you're struggling to let go of past hurts too. Some of the icky, nagging reminders keep showing up, whether you want them to or not. You do your best to press them down, but they pop up again, and often at the worst times. When your best friend announces her pregnancy. When a coworker celebrates a new romance. When your cousin gets a big job promotion.

Oops. There's that nagging cough again.

Perhaps this is why the writer of Proverbs so aptly said, "Fix your gaze before you." When you spend too much time looking over your shoulder, nothing good comes of it!

> *I'll keep my eyes fixed on the here and now, Lord!*
> *Thank You for that reminder. Amen.*

PRAYER JAR INSPIRATION:

I can "fix" my gaze and not fret over yesterday or tomorrow.

GROWING STRONGER

"Nevertheless, the righteous will hold to their ways,
and those with clean hands will grow stronger."

JOB 17:9 NIV

Have you ever been on a long road trip with kids in the car? If so, you've probably heard the question: "Are we there yet?" To you, the road trip is part of the fun and adventure. To the kids, though? Not so much!

If you're traveling out of a season of past hurts, no doubt you're anxious to hit the road and put that old town or city behind you. You're asking God, "Are we there yet?" and He's asking you to look around you and appreciate the journey that takes you out of that old place.

So, take a moment to do just that. Instead of trying to rush God, offer up a prayer of thanks that the place you're in today doesn't look like the place you were in yesterday. Your minivan is pointed in a more hopeful direction now. You're growing stronger.

And even though the journey might be taking longer than you expected, you are well on your way, with a brand-new spiritual GPS that's guaranteed to get you to your destination on God's perfect timeline.

The road might be long, Lord, but I'm in a better
place than I was. Thank You for that! Amen.

PRAYER JAR INSPIRATION:

With God's help, I am growing stronger.

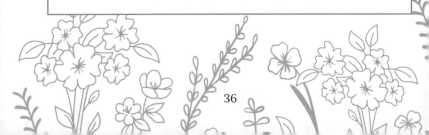

FORGET THE FORMER THINGS

"Forget the former things; do not dwell on the past. See, I am doing a new thing! Now it springs up; do you not perceive it?"

ISAIAH 43:18–19 NIV

One good thing about yesterday is that it's, well. . .*yesterday*. It's not today. *Yester* means "last past," after all.

Still, some people live today as if they're still stuck in yesterday. *Today* means "this present day." It's pretty specific, isn't it?

Really, "today" is a mentality. That mentality includes phrases like "fresh start," "new beginnings," and "new outlook." And guess what happens when you drag yesterday into today? You forget those phrases. You get selective amnesia. You're not feeling that fresh start, which means hope has no place to reside.

Give hope a chance to blossom by living in today. Yester is no more. So forget the former things. Don't dwell on the past. God is doing a brand-new thing!

I'm so grateful that "yester" is behind me,
Lord! Thank You for today. Amen.

PRAYER JAR INSPIRATION:

I won't dwell in the past.

NO MORE

For I will forgive their wickedness and will remember their sins no more.

HEBREWS 8:12 NIV

Moving forward from shame or regret can be difficult. One reason so many of us feel shame is because the actions of yesterday don't line up with our morality (or Spirit-infused beliefs) today. The shackles of what we did "back then" are shameful.

And those things probably are shameful, but Jesus was clear that we're not to carry guilt and shame. One of the most amazing things about His grace is that it completely covers our shame. It's a free ocean of forgiveness and mercy, wide enough to wash away those feelings associated with shame and regret.

Everyone makes mistakes. But what bliss to move into the freedom of healing in Christ. No matter what you did back then, you don't have to live in the past anymore. You are a new creation in Christ Jesus. Live like it!

*You remember my sins no more, Jesus, so I will do my
best to let go of the shame associated with them. Amen.*

PRAYER JAR INSPIRATION:

I am a new creation. Old things have passed away.

38

IT'S A PROCESS

And I am sure of this, that he who began a good work in you
will bring it to completion at the day of Jesus Christ.

PHILIPPIANS 1:6 ESV

Consider the word *process*. It can be used as either a verb or a noun. When you *process* something, you think long and hard about it. You examine it carefully from every angle. But when you use *process* as a noun (e.g., "It's a process"), the word takes on a whole new meaning.

Whether you use the word as a verb or a noun, there's an implication of time. "Process" doesn't happen instantly. It requires effort and patience as things progress. (Funny how similar process and progress are.)

In other words, no matter what you're processing today, it's going to be a process. But here's a promise in the middle of the process: the same God who started a good work in you is going to be faithful to complete it. He is not giving up, and neither should you.

You started a good work in me, Jesus, and I know You're
going to see it through. Thank You! Amen.

PRAYER JAR INSPIRATION:

I can trust God with the process.

39

DON'T REHEARSE IT

And he who was seated on the throne said, "Behold,
I am making all things new." Also he said, "Write this
down, for these words are trustworthy and true."

REVELATION 21:5 ESV

Whenever you replay something (sharing the story with a friend, for example), you're bringing it to the forefront of your thoughts again. And the more friends you share your story with, the harder it becomes to put the past in the past where it belongs.

Some people make their tragic past their full identity. They rehearse the story over and over. It's one thing to share your testimony; it's another thing altogether to constantly bring up how badly you were hurt by someone because you're looking for ongoing empathy.

The past hurt you. That part is obvious to all who know you and know your story. But if you camp out there, if you identify as that hurt person, then your current friends will always tiptoe around you. They won't relax and be themselves.

It's great to share your testimony, but if it has become altogether different than a praise report, you might need to reanalyze who (and how often) you share. Just something to ponder as you heal from the traumas of yesterday.

I won't rehearse it, Jesus! I've rehashed that story enough
already! With Your help, I can put it behind me. Amen.

PRAYER JAR INSPIRATION:

Rehearsal is over! I'm putting the past in the past where it belongs!

I SHALL

Heal me, O LORD, and I shall be healed; save me,
and I shall be saved, for you are my praise.

JEREMIAH 17:14 ESV

If you've ever been in a car accident and suffered broken bones or other injuries, healing can take weeks or months. Sometimes the injuries are so complex that they require several surgeries and extended hospital stays.

If you're dealing with multiple injuries at once, each must heal in its own time and its own way. A broken femur, a ruptured spleen, deep lacerations in your arm—even one of these would be enough to cause pain and distress. But all happening simultaneously? It can be overwhelming. A good doctor would say, "Let's deal with each issue individually." And that's good advice, whether you're dealing with physical or emotional wounds.

Sometimes you're so overwhelmed with injuries from your past that the whole of it can overwhelm you. You don't know where—or if—healing will begin.

Now look at these things considering today's scripture: "Heal me, O LORD, and I shall be healed." The process of healing is, indeed, a process. But you can trust Him every step of the way.

I'm so glad the healing process has begun, Lord! Amen.

PRAYER JAR INSPIRATION:

I shall be healed. And I'll trust Jesus every step of the way.

FREEDOM!

Live as free people, but do not use your freedom
as a cover-up for evil; live as God's slaves.

1 PETER 2:16 NIV

Would you consider yourself a forgetful person? Have you ever forgotten someone's birthday? What about bills? Ever forget to pay one? There's nothing worse than neglecting to pay the electric bill or car payment!

Sometimes life is so crazy busy that we get overwhelmed and overlook basic things. (What else would explain that time you showed up at work wearing mismatched shoes?)

If ordinary daily tasks are so easy to forget, why do you suppose we have such a hard time forgetting the past? Even if we're able to heal from it, forgetting is another thing altogether!

The Bible says that God forgets our sins once we repent. As far as the east is from the west—that's how far our sins are removed from us.

If God can forgive and forget the past, maybe we need to work harder at letting it go. Clearly He doesn't want us to dwell there! (Why go on living in the desert when you've been offered the promised land?)

Step into the promised land, friend. Forget yesterday. Live for today!

The promised land sounds mighty good to me, Lord!
I can't wait to cross the Jordan! Amen.

PRAYER JAR INSPIRATION:

I choose freedom!

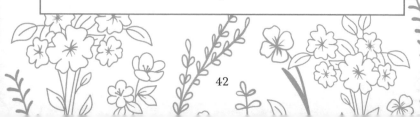

FORGET THE FORMER THINGS

"Remember not the former things, nor consider the things of old."

ISAIAH 43:18 ESV

Have you ever heard of phantom pain? Sometimes people who've lost limbs still claim to feel pain in the area where that limb used to be.

Other times you have "reminder" pains. Maybe during a bad storm, the ankle you broke ten years ago randomly begins to ache. You feel the pain shooting through you like an electric shock.

The body is fascinating. It has a hard time letting go of the pain of yesterday. And the heart is much the same.

In many ways, those phantom pains are a lot like what we feel in our hearts when an emotional storm comes or we're reminded of the pains of yesterday. We feel it all over again, as if it's just happening.

Today God wants to remind you that phantom pains are just that—phantom. They're the enemy's vain attempt to draw you back into that valley where you once lived. But you've already made up your mind: you're not going back there. Living in the sunlight is a much better option. Yesterday can't hurt you anymore.

Jesus, thank You for brushing away
phantom pains when they come. Amen.

PRAYER JAR INSPIRATION:

Phantom pain can't really hurt me unless I give it a place to dwell.

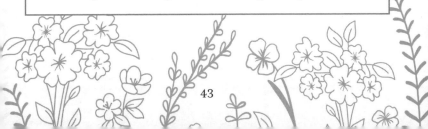

A TIMELY WORD

*The Lord God has given me the tongue of those who are
taught, that I may know how to sustain with a word
him who is weary. Morning by morning he awakens;
he awakens my ear to hear as those who are taught.*

ISAIAH 50:4 ESV

Think of a time when you were in intense physical pain. Maybe you had kidney stones or labor pains. The pain gripped you in a way you couldn't properly deal with. All you wanted was relief—at any cost.

There are people out there who are in so much pain that they want release from it—at any cost. There are warning signs if you keep your eyes wide open. God wants you to be a light to those who have reached this point. You never know when a timely word will change everything in a person's situation.

So, how does this work? Instead of saying, "This really stinks!" say something like, "I'm looking forward to the day when this is behind you." Instead of saying, "This is so unfair," say something like, "How can I help?"

You can help, and often it requires simply being there with a person as they work their way through the valley. Be that kind word in due season. Offer hope.

Show me what to say to those who are truly struggling, Lord. Amen.

PRAYER JAR INSPIRATION:

I can speak a timely word and change someone's life forever.

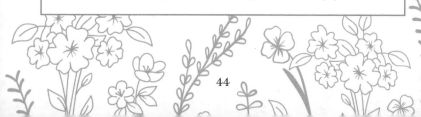

I DON'T WANT A REPEAT

*Now the Lord is the Spirit, and where the Spirit
of the Lord is, there is freedom.*

2 CORINTHIANS 3:17 NIV

The reason so many of us get stuck in the past is because we're terrified of a repeat in the present. We put walls up and walk around guarded because we're so afraid to trust again. Or to love again. Or to walk in close relationship with a friend again.

We have a "been there, done that" attitude that puts protective barriers around our hearts.

If you've been hurt by a friend or loved one in the past, it can be hard to trust again. But part of the journey out of that pain is the recognition that not all people are alike. Not all men are alike. Not all friends are alike. Not all preachers are alike. Not all churches are alike.

We must stop lumping people into groups and making assumptions, and that can happen only when we become vulnerable once again.

And remember, there's freedom in Christ. That's not just a saying. There's literal, actual freedom. Where the Spirit of the Lord is, there *is* freedom! Be set free from the past today!

*You are my answer, Jesus! In You, I can find freedom.
There will be no repeats from the past. It's all behind me
now, and I have You to thank for that. Amen.*

PRAYER JAR INSPIRATION:

No repeats from the past for me, Lord!

INSTANT REPLAY

Whoever dwells in the shelter of the Most High will rest in the shadow of the Almighty. I will say of the LORD, "He is my refuge and my fortress, my God, in whom I trust."

PSALM 91:1–2 NIV

When you're watching a ball game on TV, you have the benefit of instant replay for questionable calls. Say a player slides into third base and the ump cries, "Out!" Only instant replay shows otherwise. He was clearly safe.

You don't have the benefit of seeing your past through a slow, precise lens. No doubt you've solidified memories in your brain one way when, in fact, they might not be that way at all.

This is one of the chief reasons you need to learn to let go of past hurts. Some of your memories could be skewed. Perhaps some of the things you're hanging on to didn't happen exactly as you remember.

No matter how things went in the past, God has marked you "safe" today. The haunts of yesterday aren't here to torment you anymore. There's a reason they call it the past. Yesterday has passed, after all.

You are my refuge and fortress, Jesus. I'm truly safe with You.

PRAYER JAR INSPIRATION:

Safety is always a given for a child of God.

HEALING
IN RELATIONSHIPS

Have you ever experienced a broken relationship? Maybe your actions or words hurt someone you love. Now you are filled with stress and regret, wondering how you can make it better. Or maybe someone you loved and trusted took advantage of you or said hurtful things. How will you ever find the strength to forgive them? How will you ever move on?

James 5:16 (NKJV) says, "Confess your trespasses to one another, and pray for one another, that you may be healed. The effective, fervent prayer of a righteous man avails much."

At times like these, we need to turn to God for guidance. God's Word advises us, when restoring a broken relationship, to be humble, offer forgiveness, communicate well, and have patience through the process. Here are some Bible verses that can help during difficult times of healing:

Remain humble: *"With all lowliness and gentleness, with long-suffering, [bear] with one another in love, endeavoring to keep the unity of the Spirit in the bond of peace"* (Ephesians 4:2–3 NKJV).

Offer forgiveness: *"And be kind to one another, tenderhearted, forgiving one another, even as God in Christ forgave you"* (Ephesians 4:32 NKJV).

Communicate well: *"So then, my beloved brethren, let every man be swift to hear, slow to speak, slow to wrath"* (James 1:19 NKJV).

Have patience: *"Be joyful in hope, patient in affliction, faithful in prayer"* (Romans 12:12 NIV).

HE WILL USE IT FOR HIS GLORY

Blessed is the man who remains steadfast under trial,
for when he has stood the test he will receive the crown
of life, which God has promised to those who love him.

JAMES 1:12 ESV

You thought that friendship would last forever. You were BFFs from the moment you met. But something went terribly wrong, and now you're heartbroken. The hours of late-night chats. The shared secrets. The silly giggles and laughs over nonsensical things.

Letting go of a relationship, especially one you enjoyed for years, can be devastating. And heartbreaking. It takes a supernatural move of God to bring comfort to your broken heart after losing a good friend.

No matter what has happened, God will bring comfort, hope, and peace once again. He will. That heart of yours will heal over time. And no doubt you'll learn some lessons—however hard—about the next friendship that comes your way. In some ways you're sadder, but you're wiser.

God will use this situation for your benefit and for His glory. He always does. So go ahead and grieve, but anticipate healing. It's just around the corner. And remember, Jesus is a friend who sticks closer than a brother. That's one friendship that will never end.

I anticipate healing, Jesus. Amen.

PRAYER JAR INSPIRATION:

No matter what, God will use my situation for His glory.

THE BIBLICAL WAY

*Therefore confess your sins to each other and pray for
each other so that you may be healed. The prayer of
a righteous person is powerful and effective.*

JAMES 5:16 NIV

It feels impossible. There's been a breach in your friendship. You haven't spoken in weeks. But there's a nudging in your heart that somehow things could mend if you would just set a plan in motion. But you're clueless about what that plan should look like.

So you pray. You give the situation to God. You ask for healing to mend the rift. Then He encourages you to reach out with a text. Just a few words: I MISS YOU.

And you wait. Time passes. And then a response comes: I MISS YOU TOO.

It's a start. You draw a deep breath and issue an apology for any role you might have played in the broken places. She responds in kind. And soon you're talking about the kids, the upcoming vacation, all the usual things.

Broken relationships aren't always going to mend. Sometimes God separates you from people for your own protection. But there are still situations where you know in your heart that the friendship isn't truly over yet. So leave the door cracked if you feel that nudge from the Spirit. He'll show you what to do.

I trust You, Jesus. If the door is meant to swing wide, it will. Amen.

PRAYER JAR INSPIRATION:

I can't fix broken relationships, but Jesus can.

LET GO OF THE
SCENT OF DEATH

*"He will wipe away all tears from their eyes.
There will be no more death, no more grief or
crying or pain. The old things have disappeared."*
REVELATION 21:4 GNT

Imagine opening the garage door and finding a dead mouse inside. From the looks of things, he's been there awhile. He's stiff and cold. And there's an odor. A bad one.

You do your best to clean it up, but even after bleaching the area, you still smell that lingering scent of death in the air.

This might seem like an extreme example, but that's kind of what it's like when you refuse to allow healing to come. Death takes its place. Rigor takes its place. And before long, there's a "scent" about you that others notice.

Oh, you do your best to cover it up, but it's there, nonetheless.

It's time to let go of unforgiveness, friend. It's time to let go of anger. It's time to give your broken heart, your errant thoughts, to Jesus once and for all. He will give those icky things a proper funeral, and no scent of death will remain. When the Bible says, "The old things have disappeared," it means everything, even the very scent of death.

*Jesus, I'm ready for the funeral to take place so that these
things that have plagued me will be a thing of the past.*

PRAYER JAR INSPIRATION:

I won't tolerate the smell of death. I will ask Jesus to deal with it.

SOMETHING'S GOTTA GIVE

The vexation of a fool is known at once,
but the prudent ignores an insult.
PROVERBS 12:16 ESV

Relationships are hard, but codependent relationships are over-the-top difficult. When you're in a precarious friendship where the other person has an unhealthy attachment to you, situations can get tricky.

You want to be a good friend. You've tried. But she's consuming you. Draining you. Accusing you of not being caring enough, no matter how much you give. And you're about to reach the breaking point. Should you cut off the friendship altogether?

You weren't meant to fix everything. If you sweep in and play the role that only God should play, your friend will never learn anything. You have to take steps backward from the friendship until she gets the message that you're not her be-all, end-all.

It's not going to be easy, but when relationships reach the codependent stage, something has to give. So take this as a sign. Back away from the fire—for your safety and your loved one's, as well.

Show me what to do with the tough ones, Jesus! Amen.

PRAYER JAR INSPIRATION:

I'm not the fixer of all things. But my God is.

ALL TANGLED UP

*"And when you stand and pray, forgive anything you
may have against anyone, so that your Father in
heaven will forgive the wrongs you have done."*

MARK 11:25 GNT

Have you ever tried to run a hairbrush through a little girl's hair?
Maybe you hit a spot with a giant tangle and the child started to cry.
There's only one way to untangle hair—gently. Slowly. Usually you
work your way up from the bottom.

Some friendships are like that tangled hair. It's going to take time
and patience to unravel the mess, and there may be a little crying along
the way. (Hey, no one said healing was easy! It's a process.)

Think about the last time you reached for a string of Christmas
lights from a storage box and found them all twisted up. It took a
while to get them separated, but once you did, they shimmered as
brightly as ever.

That's how relationships are too. Take the time to heal correctly,
and in the end all tangles will be gone, all twists and kinks will be
worked out, and the relationship will shine as never before.

*I'm going to need Your patience as we
unravel this mess together, Lord! Amen.*

PRAYER JAR INSPIRATION:

*Tangled messes don't have to be permanent.
They can be untangled with patience and hard work.*

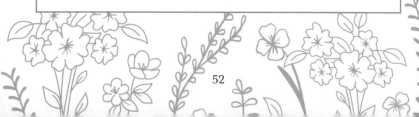

LIVE AT PEACE
WITH EVERYONE

If it is possible, as far as it depends on you, live at peace with everyone.
ROMANS 12:18 NIV

Have you ever watched a litter of puppies at play? They're having so much fun, tossing and turning, yipping at one another. Until one of them decides to bare his teeth. Then all bets are off! Before you know it, the whole pack is in a squabble, and they don't stop until their owner steps in.

Sometimes that's how friend groups are. You all get along great. You play together. You eat together. You even worship together. Then someone decides to stir up trouble. Before you know it, the whole friend group is going at it.

It's hard to reconcile with one person, let alone a whole friend group! That's why it's important to be a peacemaker when you can.

Look at today's verse. Focus on the words "*as far as it depends on you.*"

God knew it wouldn't be easy. But you really can be a peacemaker, even when the rest of your friends are squabbling!

You see to the very heart of my friend groups, Jesus.
Help me to be the best friend I can be and to be a
peacemaker to the best of my ability. Amen.

PRAYER JAR INSPIRATION:

Just because everyone else is squabbling doesn't mean I have to.

GRACE AND MERCY

*If we confess our sins, he is faithful and just to forgive us
our sins and to cleanse us from all unrighteousness.*

1 JOHN 1:9 ESV

Grace and mercy—two things you hope others will extend to you when you mess up. A little grace covers a lot. And those who extend mercy to the ones who've hurt them? Those are some amazing people right there!

Here's the thing: God doesn't just want you to receive grace and mercy. He wants you to extend it to others, even the ones who've hurt you. He's not asking you to be a doormat, but there are situations where you should probably just forgive the person who hurt you and let it go, especially if she has asked for your forgiveness and tried to make things right.

Why is it so important to forgive and offer grace? Because God forgives. . .as you forgive. If you don't let it go, then He doesn't have to let your sins go either.

That's pretty heavy stuff, but it's what the Bible says. So choose grace. Choose a merciful response to the ones who've wounded you. Then watch as God pours mercy and grace out on you too!

*It's not easy, but today I will choose to extend
grace to the ones who've hurt me, Jesus. Amen.*

PRAYER JAR INSPIRATION:

Grace and mercy are gifts I can offer to others.

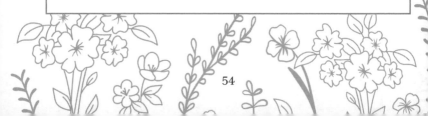

SPEAK THE
TRUTH IN LOVE

*Instead, by speaking the truth in a spirit of love, we must
grow up in every way to Christ, who is the head.*

EPHESIANS 4:15 GNT

You're watching a friend go down the wrong path. You know she's on a course that's heading for a cliff. And you try to tell her, but she's not listening. Instead, defiant, she holds up her hand and says, "Let me live my own life."

And you have. You've backed away. You've prayed. You've given her space. But it's obvious she's on a course that won't end well.

So what do you do? Do you try once more to intervene, to bring healing to her heart and your relationship? Or do you walk away completely?

Though it might seem impossible, you might want to try one more time to speak the truth. You can do so in love, with her well-being at the forefront of the conversation. If she still won't receive it, then, for your own protection, it might be good to step away from the relationship—at least for now. You don't want her to drag you down with her.

It's not unkind to speak hard truth. In fact, it's more unkind not to. So, deep breath. Let's give this one more shot!

*I don't know why I'm so nervous to speak the truth,
Jesus. Please give me courage and peace. Amen.*

PRAYER JAR INSPIRATION:

*Kindness and truthfulness go hand in hand.
I can be both kind and truthful.*

IT'S NOT TOO LATE TO HEAL

Cast your burden on the Lord, and he will sustain you;
he will never permit the righteous to be moved.

PSALM 55:22 ESV

Do you have relational issues that go back to childhood? Maybe you had a deadbeat dad who left the family never to return. Or maybe you had a sibling who did something cruel to hurt your family—something that had devastating consequences.

It's hard to recover from childhood relational traumas. As a little one, you simply didn't have the tools necessary to mend the heartbreak caused by others, especially adults.

Now here you are, an adult yourself, having to make adult decisions. But the lingering pain caused long ago by people has left its mark.

It's not too late to heal. You may never see that person again. (Or you might.) But the truth is, God can bring complete and total healing to your heart and give you the tools you need, not only to forgive, but to live in freedom. You don't have to repeat the patterns learned as a child. You can walk in liberty from now on, completely healed from the past.

I'm so glad I don't have to worry about the pain of yesterday,
Jesus. I don't have to repeat the patterns taught to me as a
child. You've set me free, and I'm so grateful. Amen.

PRAYER JAR INSPIRATION:

I can live in the freedom of Christ.

PATIENCE, FRIEND!

It is better to be patient than powerful. It is better to
win control over yourself than over whole cities.

PROVERBS 16:32 GNT

We live in a world filled with people who have different personalities and different belief systems. What's perfectly acceptable and normal to one person might be taboo to another. It's hard to know how to communicate effectively with so many different perspectives at play.

This is particularly hard when you're thrown into a situation where you have no choice but to play nice with one another. At work, say. Maybe you've been placed on a team with someone who rubs you the wrong way. You're doing your best, but the other person sure doesn't make it easy.

Relational issues can reach the boiling point if we don't respond kindly. But God can bring healing even in the toughest work-related relationship if you ask Him to be at the center of it. And remember, a little patience goes a long, long way when you're trying to figure out how best to communicate.

Show me how to be patient with others, Jesus.
It's not easy, so I'll need Your help for sure. Amen.

PRAYER JAR INSPIRATION:

It is better to be patient than powerful.

PUZZLING RELATIONSHIPS

*By the authority of our Lord Jesus Christ I appeal to
all of you, my friends, to agree in what you say, so that
there will be no divisions among you. Be completely
united, with only one thought and one purpose.*

1 Corinthians 1:10 gnt

Some relationships are like puzzles. So many pieces are scattered everywhere, you don't know how or if things will come together properly. Let's face it: people are difficult. Even in churches people can get hurt. They all start out on the same team but end up at one another's throats. It's crazy.

Maybe you've been through a rough season at your church. Perhaps someone you thought was a friend talked badly about you behind your back or betrayed a confidence. Now you're not sure if you even want to go back to that place where the pain took place.

A lot of people walk away from churches over issues like this, and Satan (the enemy of our souls) is thrilled and delighted when they do. That's his ultimate goal, after all, to bring division and pain.

No matter how badly you've been hurt by a church member, please don't turn and run. The Bible provides clear instruction for how to mend those situations. God is honored when we follow His plan and when relationships between believers are mended.

*I will do my best to live at peace, especially
inside the walls of my church. Amen.*

PRAYER JAR INSPIRATION:

I will subvert the enemy's tactics when he attempts to divide.

LOVER OF MY SOUL

"The LORD appeared to him from far away. I have loved you with an everlasting love; therefore I have continued my faithfulness to you."

JEREMIAH 31:3 ESV

Romance movies have given us a somewhat unrealistic expectation of life. We imagine that Prince Charming will be waiting around the next corner, ready to make all things right. He's going to sweep in at just the right time and say just the right thing, and all will be well.

Sometimes it works out like that, and we meet the perfect person to share life with. Other times things go catastrophically wrong and we feel we've been cheated of the fairy tale. The person we thought we could trust turns out to be a villain in the story, not a hero. It happens.

If you've been hurt in a romantic relationship—a marriage, a dating relationship, an engagement—you are certainly not alone. And perhaps (like many), you're tempted to back away from future possibilities because of past hurts.

That's understandable, but it's not always God's best for you. He wants you to lift your eyes and look forward, not back. Maybe Mr. Right is waiting around the next bend. Maybe he's not. But you know who's right there with His hand in yours? Jesus. And He's the lover of your soul!

Thank You for loving me through all my relationships, Jesus.

PRAYER JAR INSPIRATION:

I have the best relationship a person could ever ask for—with Jesus!

RE-

For I want you to know how great a struggle I have for you and for those at Laodicea and for all who have not seen me face to face, that their hearts may be encouraged, being knit together in love, to reach all the riches of full assurance of understanding and the knowledge of God's mystery, which is Christ, in whom are hidden all the treasures of wisdom and knowledge.

COLOSSIANS 2:1–3 ESV

Have you ever examined the word *relationship*? To be in relationship with someone means you're bound to them, or are in some way related (by blood, friendship, or something else).

Now ponder the prefix *re-*. *Re-* means again. Words like *rebuild, redo, readjust, recommit* all start with this tiny prefix. So does the word *relationship*.

Could it be that God, in His infinite wisdom, is trying to convey a not-so-subtle message here? Relationships, after all, must be revisited (another *re-* word). You have to reanalyze them from time to time to make sure they're healthy.

Part of the healing that comes from broken relationships starts with the willingness to go back to the beginning and look once more at where you started with this person. Maybe it's time to reassess those friendships so that they can move forward in peace.

> *Soften my heart so that I'm willing to revisit*
> *the places You want me to go, Lord. Amen.*

PRAYER JAR INSPIRATION:

God has offered me many redos in our relationship. And I am thankful!

RELATING

The unfolding of your words gives light;
it gives understanding to the simple.
PSALM 119:130 NIV

What does it mean to "relate" to something? Maybe your friend tells a story about how she had a hard time sticking to her dieting while at a family reunion and you say, "I relate to that!"

When you relate it means, "I've been there too. I understand. I really do."

Now think of that word in relation to the people you're related to. You're "related" to them, but do you "relate" to them?

Part of the problem with twenty-first-century relationships is that we don't take the time to relate to one another. We buzz by one another on our way somewhere else and pretty much coexist without really relating.

Today, take the time to relate with your relations. No, *really*. Ask questions. Dig deep. Bake some cookies together. Offer to help in some unexpected ways. You might forge deeper relationships if you pause and take the time to be there: physically, emotionally, and spiritually. In doing so, you're saying, "I get it. I understand."

Show me how best to relate to the people
You've placed in my path, Lord! Amen.

> ### PRAYER JAR INSPIRATION:
> *To relate is to understand.*

GO FIRST

Bear with each other and forgive one another if any of you has a grievance against someone. Forgive as the Lord forgave you.

COLOSSIANS 3:13 NIV

Sometimes relationships hit a wall because neither party is willing to apologize first. Maybe you've said things like, "Well, if she would just come to me and say I'm sorry, I would forgive her and we could move on."

The problem is, she's probably saying the same thing.

You've heard the phrase "Be the bigger person," no doubt. It does take courage (and humility) to be the first to say you're sorry. But when you do, you open the door to healing in the relationship. And isn't that more important than holding fiercely to your stubborn pride? (Why yes, it is!)

Be the first. Even if time has passed and it's awkward. Those first few words won't be easy, but they will be life-changing for both of you. (Hint: if meeting in person is too hard, why not send a lovely email or text or handwritten letter?)

Pray about it and ask God to show you the perfect way to nudge the door open. When it comes to forgiveness, He's the pro!

It's not easy to humble myself, Lord,
but with Your help, I can do it! Amen.

PRAYER JAR INSPIRATION:

When relationships are hard, I can be the bigger person.

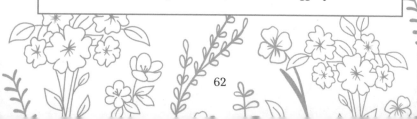

UNAVOIDABLE

Be kind to one another, tenderhearted,
forgiving one another, as God in Christ forgave you.
EPHESIANS 4:32 ESV

Not all tough relationships are avoidable. If you're a caregiver for your elderly parent with Alzheimer's, for instance, you don't have the luxury of pulling away when they lash out at you.

In circumstances like these (especially if you have a long history of abuse from that parent), you must look past some of the hard things to the pain and frustration your loved one is experiencing.

When you get to the point where you can empathize with their plight, it helps a lot in how you manage the hard days. On those days, grace plays an even bigger role—both God's grace over the situation and the amount of grace you're able to extend to your loved one.

Instead of begging God for a way out, begin to ask Him for a way through it. He hasn't promised to relieve you of pain in this life, but He has promised that He will be there beside you all the way.

I just want to run away sometimes, Lord. But I'll stay
put and do what You've called me to do. Amen.

PRAYER JAR INSPIRATION:

Struggles are unavoidable, but God is always there in each one.

63

AGREE TO DISAGREE

*Get rid of all bitterness, passion, and anger. No more shouting
or insults, no more hateful feelings of any sort. Instead, be
kind and tender-hearted to one another, and forgive one
another, as God has forgiven you through Christ.*

Ephesians 4:31–32 gnt

Politics. Religion. How to raise children. These can be very divisive topics—especially that first one. And there are hot seasons where tempers are flaring on both sides of the aisle. No doubt you've read stories of twentysomethings who ended relationships with their parents over differing political affiliations. It's sad, but these things happen.

Even inside the church, people disagree. There are dozens of theological viewpoints over hot-button topics. Maybe you've even witnessed a fight or two inside the walls of your church over doctrinal issues or music choices.

People fight. And every single person wishes that every other single person believed the way they believe. (Can you imagine what the world would be like if we were all the same? How boring!)

When it comes to disagreements, there's a simple way to put an end to strife. Agree to disagree. Say to your friend or loved one: "We don't agree on this, but I still love you and will *always* love you, no matter what." These words will be healing balm.

I will do my best to keep the waters calm, Lord. Amen.

PRAYER JAR INSPIRATION:

Just because others overreact doesn't mean I have to.

EXHAUSTION:
SLOWING DOWN
TO HEAL

Dealing with emotional, spiritual, and physical pain can be exhausting. It takes time to heal. If you're sick, you must rest and follow the doctor's instructions while you heal. If you have a broken leg, you need to stay off it and keep it elevated as much as possible.

In desperation to relieve the emotional pain they feel, some people use distraction to keep from focusing on the thing that happened to them. They stay busy to avoid thinking about it or having to deal with it.

Isaiah 40:31 (NKJV), reminds us, "But those who wait on the Lord shall renew their strength; they shall mount up with wings like eagles, they shall run and not be weary, they shall walk and not faint."

Sometimes it may feel like no one cares about the pain and scars we have from our past, but the Bible tells us that God cares. Matthew 6:26 (NKJV) reminds us of how much the Lord cares and what He will do for us: "Look at the birds of the air, for they neither sow nor reap nor gather into barns; yet your heavenly Father feeds them. Are you not of more value than they?"

If we want to fully heal, we must learn to wait on God. He will not fail. He will give us the strength to move forward and heal if we slow down and wait on Him.

BE STILL

"The Lord will fight for you; you need only to be still."
EXODUS 14:14 NIV

You're always on the go, moving a hundred miles an hour. And the troubles that plague you? Well, you drown them out with activity. Go, go, go. Rush, rush, rush. Before long, you can barely remember the things that were troubling you. To you, that's a good thing. But to God? Well, He would prefer you heal from the inside out, and that's impossible when you don't slow down.

When you buzz along at lightning speed, there's no time to do the deep intense work on your heart to heal. So you pretend. You just keep going. No one can tell the difference if you keep that smile plastered on your face.

Only God wants you to stop. He needs you to stop so that He can do a deep work. It won't be easy. It will take time. But once you've done the hard work, you won't have to pretend anymore. You won't have to fill the hours with distractions. You can settle in. . .and just be.

I'm ready to stop running from the pain, Jesus. Ready to stop
pretending. Slow me down so I can heal, I pray. Amen.

PRAYER JAR INSPIRATION:

Faster isn't always better. More isn't always more.

HE MAKES ME LIE DOWN IN GREEN PASTURES

The LORD is my shepherd, I lack nothing. He makes me lie down in green pastures, he leads me beside quiet waters, he refreshes my soul. He guides me along the right paths for his name's sake.

PSALM 23:1–3 NIV

We don't always feel like slowing down. Sometimes slowing down forces us to confront the issues we've been avoiding.

Maybe the psalmist understood this when he penned the phrase "He makes me lie down in green pastures."

Why do you suppose God had to "make" him lie down? Interesting question, right? Until we slow down, we don't have the headspace (or the heart space) to do the hard work that we need to do to heal. Busy people aren't healing on the go, after all.

Still people. Quiet people. These are healing people.

So slow down. Lie in green pastures. Rest. Reflect. Do the hard work on the inside, not just the outside. And watch as God heals you from the inside out, a true green-pasture healing.

I will be still whenever You call me to lie down, Jesus. I won't fight You on this because I know You have my well-being at heart. Amen.

PRAYER JAR INSPIRATION:

What a good, good Father, to call us to seasons of rest.

A GIANT TIME-OUT

*Now the L<small>ORD</small> provided a huge fish to swallow Jonah,
and Jonah was in the belly of the fish three days and three nights.*

J<small>ONAH</small> 1:17 NIV

Jonah probably didn't anticipate landing in the belly of huge fish. But there's no denying his own actions led him there. God instructed him to go to Nineveh. Jonah (not so graciously) declined and ran in the opposite direction, boarding a ship to Tarshish.

And that's when the trouble began. His "no" to God created a scenario that put everyone else on the ship in potential peril. A storm hit. The boat rocked. The men panicked. And everyone agreed in unison that Jonah was to blame.

So, off the boat he went, straight into the waters. And from there? Swallowed whole by a giant fish.

In the belly of the fish, Jonah had one thing he hadn't allowed himself before: time. Time to think. Time to repent. Time to pray. Time to figure out a new plan.

Maybe you've landed in the belly of a giant fish too. Don't waste the opportunity. Let God do the hard work while you're in there.

*I won't make You put me in time-out, Lord!
Hopefully I will learn my lessons the first time! Amen.*

PRAYER JAR INSPIRATION:

Repentance is key. I need to let God work in my heart.

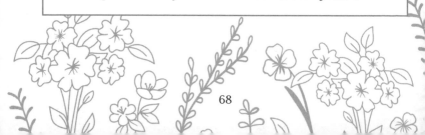

SOMETIMES IT
JUST TAKES TIME

The end of a matter is better than its beginning,
and patience is better than pride.

ECCLESIASTES 7:8 NIV

Wouldn't it be amazing if a broken bone could heal overnight? And wouldn't it be wonderful if a deep gash in your arm could be mended in an instant?

These things take time, and often lots of it! A broken arm also requires stillness to mend. Get that arm moving too much and it might take even longer for the bones to fuse back together.

God created us to heal naturally, but He deliberately chose a slower method. Why do you suppose that is? Why intentionally make us wait for healing?

The process of a bone mending is just that. . .a process. Sure, God could have set it all on warp speed, but it's mesmerizing to think about the immune system springing into action to bring about inflammation, which triggers the surrounding tissues, marrow, and blood to respond. It's all a chain reaction that leads to new bone forming at the point of the break.

Healing takes time. And it's never a good idea to rush the process. So don't push yourself to make everything perfect today. Good things come to those who wait.

I will trust Your process, Lord. Amen.

PRAYER JAR INSPIRATION:

Good things are coming—all in God's good timing.

IN THE STILLNESS

He says, "Be still, and know that I am God; I will be exalted
among the nations, I will be exalted in the earth."

PSALM 46:10 NIV

When you've had a hard day, you just want to get home, put on your pj's, and kick up your feet. There's something about slowing down that makes everything better. You're done with the chaos. You're done with the arguments. It's just you, a cup of tea, and a few minutes of peace and quiet.

God always intended healing to come in the quiet, slow spaces. Maybe that's why He instructs us to meet Him in our prayer closet, a place set apart, away from others. It's so much easier to get His perspective when the loud voices around us have quieted down.

Where do you meet with God? Do you have a special location? Maybe it's time to create a set-apart place where you can have your quiet time with Him.

A favorite chair. The back patio. Your recliner. The bathtub. Any and all of these places will do. Just create a mindset that things will slow down in that space so that you can focus on Him.

I want to be where You are, Jesus.
Meet me in our special place. Amen.

PRAYER JAR INSPIRATION:

My favorite place to meet with Jesus is _____.

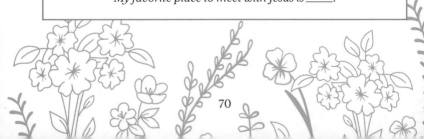

RUN THE RACE

*Therefore, since we are surrounded by so great a cloud of witnesses,
let us also lay aside every weight, and sin which clings so closely,
and let us run with endurance the race that is set before us.*

HEBREWS 12:1 ESV

When you're running a race, you have a destination in mind. You're doing everything you can to get to the finish line and win the prize. Nothing can slow you down. Your eye is fixed on the goal in front of you.

Unfortunately, life has a way of creating interruptions, and we don't always reach our goals. We make plans, and they fizzle. We set our sights on a job opportunity, and it falls through. We face disappointment when we fall short.

Today God wants to heal you from those disappointments. Who cares if things didn't go exactly as planned? You serve a heavenly Father who has His very best in mind for you. Perhaps He had something even bigger, even better, than what you had planned for yourself.

Go ahead and make goals. But don't beat yourself up when you don't hit them. Trust Him to give you something even better!

I will keep running, Jesus. But if I fall short, I won't beat myself up. Amen.

PRAYER JAR INSPIRATION:

*Disappointment isn't a reason to give up. I trust
that God has something better in store for me.*

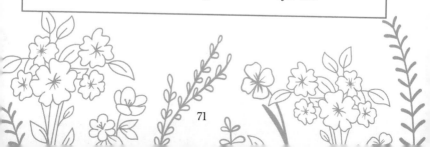

SLOW DOWN THAT TRAIN!

*Be still before the L*ord *and wait patiently for him; fret
not yourself over the one who prospers in his way,
over the man who carries out evil devices!*

Psalm 37:7 esv

Hurry! Go, go, go! Get in the car and buzz your way there, slapping on lipstick on the way. Eat that sandwich in the driver's seat. Make that business call from the car. There's no time to stop. No time to drive the speed limit when you live on the edge.

Maybe you can relate. Perhaps this is how you live: late to every important (and unimportant) event. And when you come tearing into the parking lot, your heart is racing, you have mayonnaise on your chin, and you can't find your phone—even though you just made a call.

This lifestyle is way too common in the twenty-first century, but oh the troubles that come from it. Health challenges. Emotional traumas. And worst of all, when you're always late, there's no time to heal.

This might be the hardest thing you've ever had to do, but today God is asking you to slow down that train. He has work for you to do, but it's quiet, concentrated work that requires stillness.

It's not going to be easy, but I will slow down, Lord! Amen.

PRAYER JAR INSPIRATION:

Hurry leads to worry.

72

POWER DOWN

*Be angry, and do not sin; ponder in your
own hearts on your beds, and be silent.*

PSALM 4:4 ESV

It's hard to quiet yourself long enough to heal when notifications are going off on your phone, your smart watch, and your laptop. All that ding-ding-dinging is a terrible distraction.

Let's face it: Technology can be a wonderful thing, but with music playing, movies streaming, friends texting, and bosses emailing, it can get overwhelming. You can slip into sensory overload with so many devices vying for your attention all at once.

It's time for some stillness. Turn off the ringer on that phone. Power down the laptop. Shut off the TV show. Close your eyes and just. . .be.

Sure, you might not know what to do with all that stillness if you're used to go-go-going. But God can (and does) speak during the quiet times. Listen for His still, small voice. Watch as He begins to heal you as you rest from the chaos.

*I will do my best to avoid the distractions today,
Lord. I'll close myself off from the chaos and
spend quiet, peaceful time with You. Amen.*

PRAYER JAR INSPIRATION:

I will choose to have a "powered down" day.

HE CALMS THE STORMS

He stilled the storm to a whisper; the waves of the sea were hushed. They were glad when it grew calm, and he guided them to their desired haven.

PSALM 107:29–30 NIV

Some days the troubles are so deep that you can't wade through them. An overdrawn bank account. A sick child. A pesky neighbor. An overbearing boss. Why do these things always seem to compound—one on top of the other?

If you're having a day like this, take a deep breath. If you can, tuck yourself away from people for a few minutes (even if it's in the restroom at work). In that place, God can calm the storm. Make a list of what needs to be done and put those things in a workable order. (One reason we often feel overwhelmed is because we can't determine a path of action.)

Once you've started your list, map out individual strategies for the problems you're facing. Having a written plan will help a lot. And remember, God sees you—even in the restroom with tears rolling down your cheeks. He's keenly aware of what you're going through and already sees the solutions before you do. So trust Him. Even if it feels impossible. Lift your hands and say, "Jesus, please heal this situation and mend my heart as well."

You can calm the storms in my heart,
even on the hardest day, Jesus. Amen.

PRAYER JAR INSPIRATION:

I can have God-breathed strategies in place
for dealing with hard situations.

EXPECTATIONS

Surely there is a future, and your hope will not be cut off.

PROVERBS 23:18 ESV

Pace yourself. What comes to mind when you read those words? Maybe you're a real go-getter, always racing toward the goal. You don't think about pacing yourself until your body breaks down or you end up plowing over someone on your way to the goal.

When it comes to healing, God wants you to pace yourself. It might sound disingenuous to say, "Lower your expectations" but if they're too high—if you're expecting instant gratification or healing—then you're bound to be disappointed every time.

Adjust those expectations. Pace your healing so you don't end up disappointed time and time again. "Good things come to those who wait" isn't just a platitude; it's truth. If everything came easily, you wouldn't be as grateful.

Today, take a close look at some of your current expectations. Are they a bit lofty? Are you expecting too much too fast? Are you constantly disappointed (by yourself and others) because of these unmanaged expectations? Pace yourself, friend. Good things will come. . .in time.

With Your help, Lord, I can manage my expectations. Amen.

PRAYER JAR INSPIRATION:

I can learn to pace myself with God's help.

SWEET SLEEP

If you lie down, you will not be afraid;
when you lie down, your sleep will be sweet.

PROVERBS 3:24 ESV

Have you ever wondered why God created humans to need sleep? He could have made us to function around the clock, 24/7. But instead, He chose to implement a necessary Sabbath rest. And He set an example for us by taking a full day off during creation.

The body is a wonderful thing. It self-heals as we sleep. Here are some important functions that take place while you're snoozing: Your tissues repair and grow. Your immune system receives the support it needs. Your memory is "consolidated" (meaning, the storage of memories takes place). Your hormones are regulated. Energy is restored. Body temperatures are regulated. And, most important of all, you're emotionally and physically restored.

Now you see why it's so important to get the rest you need! If you don't slow down to allow your immune system to receive support, what happens? If you plow forward and don't let your memory "consolidate," then what? If you don't receive emotional and physical restoration, how can you possibly handle the issues that crop up today?

You need sleep. Stop fighting it! Slow down and crawl under the covers for some much-needed zzzs!

Thank You for the reminder that I need rest, Jesus! Amen.

PRAYER JAR INSPIRATION:

I will treat rest as a friend.

REST IS CRITICAL

*"Come to me, all you who are weary
and burdened, and I will give you rest."*

MATTHEW 11:28 NIV

Rest feels counterproductive at times, especially if you're goal oriented. No doubt you would prefer to race toward the goal and feel accomplished at the end. But when it comes to recovery from emotional, spiritual, and psychological trauma, there are no clear-cut goals. Oh, you can try to set them, but the recovery is rocky, tumultuous, and unpredictable.

Some people would say, "Trust the process," but it's better to say, "Trust the God of the process." What you can't see, He can. What you can't predict, He can. He knows how and when you'll finally reach that invisible goal, and you really can trust Him at every step along the way.

It's important to note that Jesus Himself is the one who said, "Come to me, all you who are weary and burdened, and I will give you rest." He is the ultimate rest-giver. So, the key to finding rest is to spend time with Him.

I will come to You to find rest, Jesus. Amen.

PRAYER JAR INSPIRATION:

Jesus is my resting place.

ALLOW THE WORD TO SPEAK TO YOU

All Scripture is God-breathed and is useful for teaching,
rebuking, correcting and training in righteousness.

2 TIMOTHY 3:16 NIV

How's your Bible time going? For some people, their crazy-busy lives don't leave much time to dig deep into the Word of God. But in those pages, God still speaks.

There are times when you read a verse and it doesn't settle deep in your spirit. Then there are other times when you read that same verse and it strikes you like a bolt of spiritual lightning.

When you take the time to slow down to heal, don't forget to include Bible time. Words of wisdom in those pages will help you through every single transition in the healing process. And remember, the Bible is alive and active (see Hebrews 4:12). It didn't die out with the last apostle.

The truths in God's Word hold as much power today as they ever did. And when you take the time to apply them properly, they can also be a healing balm in time of need. So, what are you waiting for? Grab that Bible and start reading!

I'm so grateful for Your Word, Lord! Where would I be
without it? I'm thankful that I'll never have to know. Amen.

PRAYER JAR INSPIRATION:

The Word of God is alive and active!

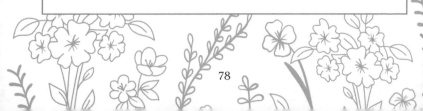

INTENTIONAL

Would not God discover this?
For he knows the secrets of the heart.

PSALM 44:21 ESV

When you do something intentionally, it means you're doing it on purpose. You've put thought into it. People use the phrase "be intentional" when they talk about things like starting diets or healing broken marriages.

People who struggle in specific areas must be intentional as well. For example, hoarders must be intentional when tackling their homes. Addicts must be intentional when dealing with alcohol or drugs.

You get the idea. Intentional means work.

Sometimes we must be intentional about slowing down. We have to treat our busyness as an addict would treat that bottle of alcohol. It's not our friend, and we have to stop inviting it to dwell with us.

Be intentional about your quiet times with God. And with simple things like rest. Sleep. Stillness. When you make up your mind to do a thing, it's more likely you will actually do it.

I want to make up my mind, Lord. I want to be more
intentional. Help me keep my focus so that I can do
this in the areas that matter most. Amen.

PRAYER JAR INSPIRATION:

Intentional = purposeful

WIPED OUT

"Come to Me, all who are weary and burdened, and I will give you rest. Take My yoke upon you and learn from Me, for I am gentle and humble in heart, and you will find rest for your souls. For My yoke is comfortable, and My burden is light."

MATTHEW 11:28–30 NASB

It's possible you're exhausted and don't even realize it. Some of the symptoms of exhaustion include chronic tiredness, headache, achy muscles, moodiness, frustration, slowed reflexes, and impaired decision-making.

If you're experiencing any of those things, you might be blaming them on something else when you're really just worn out. Hey, it happens. Sometimes people think they have the flu when they actually have sleep deprivation!

The human body wasn't built to go, go, go. God designed you to need rest so that you could think more clearly, feel good, be in an upbeat mood, and have normal, healthy reflexes. These are all important things for day-to-day living.

The only way to heal an exhausted body is to deliberately hit the Pause button. When you do. . .aah! Sweet rest makes all things better.

I will pause from my labors, Lord! Amen.

PRAYER JAR INSPIRATION:

Just because I'm a doer doesn't mean I have to be an overdoer.

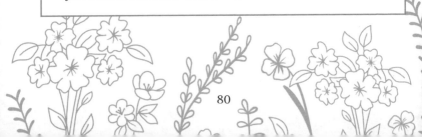

WRUNG OUT

There is a river whose streams make glad the city
of God, the holy place where the Most High dwells.

PSALM 46:4 NIV

I can't. I'm too tired.

Maybe you've used those words a time or two of late. You're not physically ill. You don't have any real symptoms to speak of. But you just can't. Your body is (as Grandma used to say) wrung out.

Think about that phrase for a moment. Back in the olden days, women would wash the laundry, then hang it on the line to dry. But sometimes clothes were too wet to dry in a timely fashion, so the ladies would wring them by hand first to get the excess water out. That way they stood a better chance of drying on the line.

When you're wrung out, it's as if life has taken you and twisted you in its hands, draining every last drop of energy. Now you're hanging out on the line, all dried out, and feeling completely useless.

The only way to fix this problem is with the kind of saturation that comes from rest and time with the Lord.

You are the stream I long to drink from, Lord! Amen.

PRAYER JAR INSPIRATION:

I can rest and refresh my soul at the river of life.

GREEN PASTURES

"I will say to the prisoners, 'Come out in freedom,' and to those in darkness, 'Come into the light.' They will be my sheep, grazing in green pastures and on hills that were previously bare."

ISAIAH 49:9 NLT

"I need a massage." "A day at the beach would do me a world of good." "I need a spa day." "A quiet evening by myself would be great for a change."

No doubt you've spoken some of these phrases over the years. There are all sorts of ways people deal with their stress and exhaustion these days.

A massage can be great, but it doesn't always get to the root of the problem. A quiet evening alone might be good too, but perhaps what you really need is the shoulder of a friend.

God wants to lead you to green pastures to recline. In green pastures, you're replenished. You don't walk away the same way you came in.

Twenty-first-century solutions (like a spa day) are fun and probably do help. . .*some.* But remember, green pastures are the places where you're called to meet with the Lord—the one who will truly restore your soul. So, while you're getting that facial or foot massage, dedicate some time to God, who's right there, waiting by still waters to be with you.

Thank You for leading me to freedom, Lord! Amen.

PRAYER JAR INSPIRATION:

What does the phrase "green pastures" look like for me?

MIND CHATTER:
HEALING FROM LIES
AND MANIPULATION

You know those consistent thoughts that run through your head when your mind moves away from whatever tasks you might be doing? Some people refer to them as "mind" or "mental" chatter. These internal conversations with ourselves are often focused on past events that were stressful. Or they could be worry about things that may happen in the future.

Some people might ask themselves during mind chatter: "Am I a failure? Am I not good enough? Why did a family member or friend treat me so badly or say harsh things to me?"

It's hard to heal when our minds recall things from our past that have caused us to hurt or feel rejected. In the dysfunctional home I grew up in, negative words were spoken more often than positive ones. It was nearly impossible to push away the negative things said to me as lies or manipulation. As an adult, I realized that it did no good to obsess about it. In fact, negative mind chatter can tear down a person and does nothing to build you up.

One of my favorite Bible verses is Philippians 4:8 (NKJV): "Finally, brethren, whatever things are true, whatever things are noble, whatever things are just, whatever things are pure, whatever things are lovely, whatever things are of good report, if there is any virtue and if there is anything praiseworthy—meditate on these things."

SET YOUR MIND ON THINGS ABOVE

Set your minds on things above, not on earthly things.
COLOSSIANS 3:2 NIV

Set your mind on things above. Sounds tricky, doesn't it? But if you've spent years giving in to negative mind chatter, it can be hard to break free.

The biblical solution is to set your mind on things above. Every time you're tempted to allow negativity to ruin your day, switch your thinking to the Lord. Come up with an easy phrase like "What would Jesus do?" It might seem silly to repeat an old phrase like this, but it forces you to refocus your attention on Him and away from your problems.

So, what would Jesus do about the situation you're walking through? How would He heal the problem you're facing? Are you more hopeful now that you've included Him in the story?

Think of it like this: When you're driving a car, do you only stare at the steering wheel? Of course not! You would crash the car. You have to cast your vision on something farther ahead to gain proper perspective.

Cast your vision on Christ today. He has all the answers you need.

Healing can come when I cast my gaze on You, Lord! Amen.

PRAYER JAR INSPIRATION:

It's possible to shift my focus to things above.

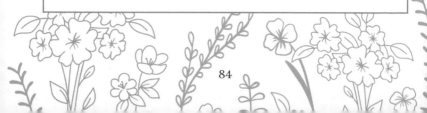

WORDS MATTER

*Therefore, as God's chosen people, holy and
dearly loved, clothe yourselves with compassion,
kindness, humility, gentleness and patience.*

Colossians 3:12 niv

Did you ever hear these words as a child? "You're so stupid!" "You're too fat." "You'll never amount to anything." "You're not as pretty as your sister." Those words stung then and still carry pain today as memories creep into your mind.

But here's the truth: Those words spoken over you as a child, the ones that wounded you and shaped your mindset? You don't have to be a slave to them any longer. Perhaps those thoughts became your reality because you didn't know any better, but now you do. Now you realize that God has so much more in mind for you.

You're beautiful. You have the mind of Christ. You'll amount to everything God has planned for you. You're an amazing child of God, loved and adored.

It's time to heal from the ugly words. The lies. The manipulation. The mean-spirited phrases that were meant to wound. Give those phrases to God. Write down on a piece of paper: "I am beautiful to my Lord. I have His mindset, His thoughts. I will go far with His help." You will, you know. Those words from yesterday can't hold you back now!

Nothing can hold me back now, Lord! Amen.

PRAYER JAR INSPIRATION:

Words can bring hurt or healing.

NO MORE MIND GAMES

I have been crucified with Christ and I no longer live,
but Christ lives in me. The life I now live in the body, I live by faith
in the Son of God, who loved me and gave himself for me.

GALATIANS 2:20 NIV

The enemy loves nothing more than to play mind games with you. He whispers negative words into your ear, and (despite your best attempts) you begin to believe them. He tells you you're unlovable. He tells you you're not as good as others. He whispers, "You'll never fit in. Why even try?"

Many of these cruel whispers have been playing on repeat since childhood. You're not sure when they started, but they're familiar. And you've been believing them for so long that changing your mindset seems impossible.

But it's not impossible. With God *all things* are possible. Even a radical change of thinking. Give your mind chatter to Him. And while you're at it, tell the enemy to get lost! He has no business messing with a child of the King, after all!

Today I give my mind chatter to You, Lord! I won't give
myself over to negative thoughts anymore. Amen.

PRAYER JAR INSPIRATION:

The enemy is a liar. God is the truth teller.

CONFUSION MUST GO!

God is not a God of confusion but a God of peace.

1 CORINTHIANS 14:33 NCV

Confusion. The word itself causes confusion. To be confused means you can't decide which is the better of the two (or three or four) choices in front of you. Confusion says, "It might be this one. Or it might be that one." Then an argument ensues in your mind as you try to reason it out.

God is not the author of confusion. The enemy is! He wants to offer you too many options, too many choices, so that your thoughts are never still.

Why does Satan want to keep you preoccupied? Because he knows that you'll never truly heal if you don't take the time to get beyond the voices in your head that tell you to do this thing or that thing.

Today, speak to that confusion in Jesus' name. Tell it to go. And in its place, God will provide supernatural peace to help you make the right choices. His choices. Healthy choices. The ones that lead to life and healing.

*Thank You for giving me direction, Lord. I don't need to
live in confusion. I can follow hard after You. Amen.*

PRAYER JAR INSPIRATION:

Confusion must go in Jesus' name!

DON'T BELIEVE THE LIES

*Do not lie to one another, seeing that you have put off the old
self with its practices and have put on the new self, which is
being renewed in knowledge after the image of its creator.*

COLOSSIANS 3:9–10 ESV

Have you ever believed a lie for so long that it felt like the truth? Think of the little girl who is told she's stupid. She begins to live out that message, opting to slack off in school. After all, why bother? If people already think she's stupid, she might as well become a self-fulfilling prophecy, right?

It happens all the time. People begin to believe the lies spoken over them and live them out as truths.

But they're not.

We've been taught not to lie, but we're not taught to avoid believing lies. It's time to realize they're both equally dangerous.

Have you been living out any lies in your life? What negative words have had an impact on the way you view yourself and others? It's not too late to turn those messages around. God is speaking life over you today. He's speaking hope. He's saying, "Believe the truth of My Word: you are a beloved child of the King!"

*Lord, please give me the ability to tell the
truth from a lie so I'm not deceived. Amen.*

PRAYER JAR INSPIRATION:

Lies have no authority over me!

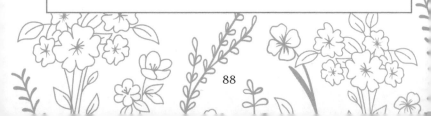

THINK ON THESE THINGS

Finally, brothers and sisters, whatever is true,
whatever is noble, whatever is right, whatever is pure,
whatever is lovely, whatever is admirable—if anything
is excellent or praiseworthy—think about such things.

PHILIPPIANS 4:8 NIV

Sometimes mind chatter can be a bit like a backed-up sink or toilet. It's clogged with so much icky stuff that you're afraid to stick the plunger in there to begin the process of unclogging.

The Bible gives the perfect tool for unclogging the spiritual and mental pipes: good thoughts. Good thoughts will purge bad ones every time. And you can prepare yourself for these attacks before they even happen.

What would it be like if you made a list (in advance) of "true" things. Noble things. Pure things. Lovely things. Admirable things. Excellent things. Praiseworthy things. What if you had an actual list to refer to whenever the enemy clogs the pipes with negativity? What if you reached for that page and began to speak aloud the goodness of God in your life?

Talk about a quick flush! That negativity would have to go when confronted with the powerful plunging truth of God's goodness in your life!

Help me guard my thoughts, Jesus. I don't want to give way
to the enemy by dwelling on impure things. Amen.

PRAYER JAR INSPIRATION:

I will think on "true" things—good things!—today.

TAKING THOUGHTS CAPTIVE

*We demolish arguments and every pretension that sets
itself up against the knowledge of God, and we take
captive every thought to make it obedient to Christ.*

2 Corinthians 10:5 NIV

Imagine you're playing Ping-Pong with a friend. When it's your time to hit the ball, you accidentally knock it across the room. Off it goes, pinging off the floor, then the wall, then a table on the far side of the room. Just about the time you think it's slowing down, it rolls under a bench, out of sight. Now you'll never be able to capture it.

Thoughts can be like that ball sometimes. You give them too much attention and they start flying. Before you know it, they're completely out of control. Worries become full-fledged fears. Small matters become huge ones. And before long you can't even remember what started it all or how to rein things in.

The Bible says you should take your thoughts captive before they start ping-ponging across the room and sweeping up all sorts of mischief. You need to squelch them when they're small, errant thoughts or they will surely try to take you to a place you were never meant to go.

You really can capture them, friend. You can demolish every single stronghold that attempts to set itself up against the knowledge of God!

Help me capture my thoughts, Lord! Amen.

PRAYER JAR INSPIRATION:

I can demolish strongholds.

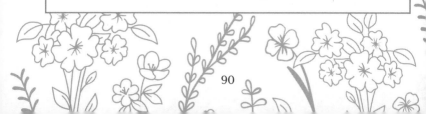

FLIP THE SWITCH

How precious to me are your thoughts, God!
How vast is the sum of them!

PSALM 139:17 NIV

Imagine you purchased a new home. Only five minutes into the move, you realized the home had a major defect: there were no light switches. None. Oh, the lights were there in every room. And they were burning bright—every single one. But there was no way to turn them off at night, so you were stuck with the glare 24/7.

In a way, your thoughts are a lot like those lights. They are burning bright in many rooms in your mind. And you've convinced yourself there's no switch. There's no way to control them. They continue to burn, burn, burn, blinding you all the while.

God's Word says otherwise. You can flip the switch and turn off those thoughts by approaching them proactively. You have the power, as a child of God, to come against those thoughts and bring them into total submission in the name of Jesus.

When we battle in the mind, we use divine weapons. We speak truth that is stronger than the lies. We build switches in every room so our minds and hearts can rest. And we do so with the assurance that God has better, bigger thoughts filled with truth and hope.

I can flip that switch with Your help, Jesus! I won't
let my thoughts control me anymore. Amen.

PRAYER JAR INSPIRATION:

Anytime I need to flip the switch so my
mind and heart can rest, I can and I will.

EXPOSURE

Have nothing to do with the fruitless deeds
of darkness, but rather expose them.

EPHESIANS 5:11 NIV

Why do you suppose God took the time during creation to separate light from darkness? He drew a very clear line between the two. In that one swift move, He was teaching us that there are two worlds, and we must choose one or the other. (Hint: He's hoping we'll choose the kingdom of light!)

God is still drawing a line between the two. Take a closer look at today's verse: "Have nothing to do with the fruitless deeds of darkness, but rather expose them."

God is in the exposing business. There are no shifting shadows with Him. He wants the light of His Word, His Son, His salvation message, to shine bright over all the dark places.

When you hover too closely to people who are living in darkness, you pull yourself into the shadows. (And then you usually end up wondering why nothing is working out in your life.)

Step out of the shadows. Come away from relationships that pull you from God. Healing only comes in the light, and you'll need to take strong, definitive steps in the direction of that light to dispel the darkness.

I'm so glad I've chosen to live in the kingdom of light, Jesus!
Thank You for always shining bright in my life. Amen.

PRAYER JAR INSPIRATION:

I can expose evil deeds of darkness by shining my light.

LET US DISCERN

"Let us discern for ourselves what is right;
let us learn together what is good."

JOB 34:4 NIV

❀❀❀

Did you know that the Holy Spirit can give you the supernatural ability to tell the truth from a lie? If you ask for that, He will surely give it. And this special gift is really going to come in handy if you're living with (or working with) someone prone to manipulation.

In some ways, manipulation is a bit like witchcraft, in that it casts a spell on the victim. But you don't have to fall under that spell any longer. With the help of the Spirit of God, you can be set free. Shackles can fall. And while you might not physically be able to walk away from a person who is attempting to manipulate you, you can most certainly learn healthy ways to deal with them.

Today, take a few minutes and ask God to endow you with the ability to discern good from evil, the truth from a lie. If a child asks his father for bread, will the father give him a stone? No. If you ask for discernment, then discernment you will surely receive.

I need discernment desperately, Lord! Sometimes it's really
hard to tell the truth from a lie. I need that ability. I don't ever
want to be confused or to listen to the wrong voices. Amen.

PRAYER JAR INSPIRATION:

With God's help, I can discern what is good.

MEMORIZE THE WORD

For the word of God is living and active, sharper than any two-edged sword, piercing to the division of soul and of spirit, of joints and of marrow, and discerning the thoughts and intentions of the heart.

HEBREWS 4:12 ESV

If you struggle with mind chatter, memorizing key Bible verses can be very helpful. When those reels begin to play in your memory, you can switch gears and begin to speak the Word over that situation.

If you're not able to memorize easily, here are a few tricks to help: Write down the Bible verses and pin or tape them in key places around your house: on your bathroom mirror, the refrigerator, your bedside table.

Here's another fun way to get the Word inside of you. Set the verses to music. Create a little melody to go along with the scripture verses you love. Go online and look for verses set to music and play them whenever you're struggling.

You can even play the audio Bible as you have a quiet rest time midday. Refocus on the promises found in the Word of God and watch that mind chatter dissipate!

There are many ways to get the Word inside of you and keep it there. Use your imagination!

I will return to Your Word, again and again, to sustain me, Lord! Amen.

PRAYER JAR INSPIRATION:

I can—and will—memorize the Word of God.

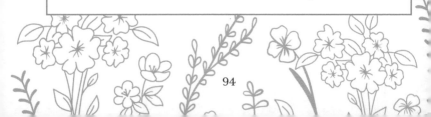

THE ENEMY'S
UPSIDE-DOWN PLAN

"You are of your father the devil, and your will is to do your father's desires. He was a murderer from the beginning, and does not stand in the truth, because there is no truth in him."

JOHN 8:44 ESV

Have you ever noticed that the enemy's lies are often the polar opposite of the Word of God? The Bible says, "Greater is He that is in me!" The devil whispers in your ear, "God doesn't care." The Bible says, "You can be victorious!" The enemy says, "You're such a failure." The Word of God is clear: "You are a beloved child of God!" The devil taunts you with "No one cares about you. You're not lovable."

Satan's upside-down plan is to attack you with lies so far-fetched that they clearly don't line up with God's promises.

And you've fallen for a few of those lies through the years, haven't you?

But no more. Once you see the enemy's schemes and tactics, you can create a battle plan. You can say, "I see what you're up to, Satan, and I'm not having it. This is what the Word of God says!" And then you pound him with the scripture. Don't stop until you begin to believe God's Word yourself.

*Thank You for the reminder that the lies of the enemy
don't have to take me down, Lord! Amen*

PRAYER JAR INSPIRATION:
I will create a plan to battle the enemy's lies.

THE ILLUSION

Abstain from every form of evil.

1 THESSALONIANS 5:22 ESV

Have you ever seen a magic show? It's hard to figure out how the magician manages to fool the audience into believing he has really cut that woman in half or made someone disappear.

The whole thing is an illusion, a trick. And the master magician is skilled in the art of making you believe one thing when it's the opposite of the truth.

Satan is the master of all magicians. He excels in the art of illusion and performs tricks that make magic shows look tame. And humans believe him. They buy into the lies.

Satan isn't content just to whisper in your ear. He sends his manipulations and lies out through social media, movies, and even the mainstream media. He gets people stirred up and convinces whole groups that something is good when, in fact, it's really bad (contrary to the Word of God).

Satan has some skills. And that's why you must have skills too. You have spiritual discernment, the holy ability to tell the truth from a lie. And it's not limited to face-to-face conversations. You can hear something online and, instead of being swept in, know that it's not true. That's how powerful spiritual discernment can be.

Thank You for the gift of discernment, Lord! Amen.

PRAYER JAR INSPIRATION:

I will not be swept into the world's tricks and deceit.

DON'T DWELL THERE

You will keep in perfect peace those whose
minds are steadfast, because they trust in you.
ISAIAH 26:3 NIV

Some people would say, "You can't control your thoughts." They do seem to flit through at lightning speed sometimes, don't they? But the Bible says you can take your thoughts captive, so clearly God wants us to aim at thought control.

Perhaps you can't control that initial thought as it breezes by, the one that says, "You're so fat and ugly. You don't look like the other women in this room." But we can stop it right there with a word from the Word: "I am wonderfully and beautifully made."

When we take the time to counteract our thoughts, we don't allow them to ruminate and grow. In other words, we don't dwell there. We don't pitch our tent on that negative idea. We act in the opposite direction. And, as we diligently fight those negative thoughts, we are overcome with God's perfect peace, which keeps our minds steadfast as we trust in Him.

My mind can be steadfast, Lord! I'll keep my
focus on You and count on Your peace! Amen.

PRAYER JAR INSPIRATION:

I will use God's holy Word to counteract my negative thoughts.

RAISE THE STANDARD!

So shall they fear the name of the Lord from the west,
and his glory from the rising of the sun. When the enemy shall come in
like a flood, the Spirit of the Lord shall lift up a standard against him.
ISAIAH 59:19 KJV

It's hard to focus when you're in a crowded (or loud) room, isn't it? You wouldn't choose a public restaurant or a ball game as a place to spend your quiet time with the Lord.

But now let's think about that idea in reverse. If the enemy is shouting loud, negative thoughts into your heart and mind, one way to counterbalance is through good noise on your end like reading scriptures aloud or singing praise songs at the top of your lungs.

The noise of truth can drown out the noise of negative mind chatter. It might seem like a momentary distraction, but distractions are good when the lies of the enemy come in like a flood.

In those moments when he's chasing hard after you, you can—with the Spirit's help—raise up a standard against the enemy.

I understand that the enemy will attempt to overtake me,
Lord; but with You on my side, I can't lose! Amen.

PRAYER JAR INSPIRATION:

God is greater and His voice is louder than the enemy's!

NO ONIONS, PLEASE

In all circumstances take up the shield of faith, with which
you can extinguish all the flaming darts of the evil one.

EPHESIANS 6:16 ESV

Imagine you're calling in an order to your favorite pizza place and you choose the supreme pizza. It comes loaded with the good stuff, but there's one thing listed that you don't want: onions. So you say, "No onions, please."

But the pizza arrives at your door with double onions. You're in a hurry (and hungry), so you shrug it off and decide to do the only thing that makes sense: pick off the onions one by one.

This might seem like a silly illustration, but this is exactly how you need to deal with those pesky negative thoughts that want to take control of your mind. Like those onions, you can pick them off, one at a time. It might feel like a nuisance, but seeing them as your enemy makes the picking worthwhile!

In a way, those thoughts are like flaming darts of the evil one. But aren't you happy to know you have a shield of faith strong enough to extinguish them!

With Your help, I can extinguish the fiery darts
the enemy sends my way, Lord. Amen.

PRAYER JAR INSPIRATION:

I can rid my mind of negative thoughts, one by one.

LIE DOWN AND SLEEP

*In peace I will both lie down and sleep; for you
alone, O Lᴏʀᴅ, make me dwell in safety.*

Psᴀʟᴍ 4:8 ᴇsᴠ

All you need is a good night's sleep, and everything will be better tomorrow. You're sure of it. So you climb into bed, pull the covers up to your chin, squeeze your eyes shut, and. . .nothing.

You can't sleep. Your mind tumbles through half a dozen conversations you had today. Regrets sweep over you as you realize you could have—*should have*—done things differently. You plan a strategy for tomorrow for how you'll make things better.

Before long, an hour has passed and you're still wide awake. Then another hour. Then you find yourself turning on the light and reaching for your phone to scroll through social media.

Mind chatter is especially difficult in the wee hours of the night. It's hard to flip the switch to turn off the day, especially if it was a troubling day. But God wants you to leave those things in His (very capable) hands. Part of trusting Him is releasing yesterday, today, and tomorrow to Him. As best as you're able, do that today.

*I will rest, Lord! I will get as much sleep as I can because I know
I will need that energy to face a brand-new day. Amen.*

PRAYER JAR INSPIRATION:

*I will sleep in peace when I release yesterday,
today, and tomorrow to God.*

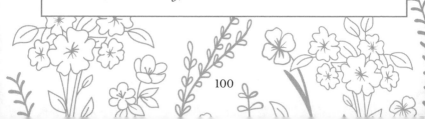

OUT OF THE PIT

Bless the Lord, O my soul, and forget not all his benefits, who forgives all your iniquity, who heals all your diseases, who redeems your life from the pit, who crowns you with steadfast love and mercy.

PSALM 103:2–4 ESV

Imagine you baked a loaf of bread a few days back and left it in plastic wrap on the counter. You're able to slice a piece of it, but you notice it has speckles of green mold on it. Ick. So you toss it into the trash can and start fresh with a new loaf.

The only way that moldy loaf of bread could actually hurt you would be if you ate it anyway. No doubt it would wreak havoc on your stomach!

That's kind of what it's like when you return to the past to consume the guilt and sins of yesterday. The past is splattered in icky green mold, with nothing good to come of it.

When God redeems your life from the pit, His ultimate goal is to set you free from the past. No more pits. No more mold. He crowns you with steadfast love and mercy to remind you daily that pit life was a stinky life. And that's not the place for you anymore.

You're a child of the King, and He has great things planned for you. Don't ever forget: He didn't just save you *from* your old life, He saved you *for* something so much better!

Thank You for giving me new life, Jesus.
You've redeemed me and set me free! Amen.

> ## PRAYER JAR INSPIRATION:
>
> *God saved me from the pit for great things!*

RUN WITH PERSEVERANCE

Therefore, since we are surrounded by such a great cloud of witnesses, let us throw off everything that hinders and the sin that so easily entangles. And let us run with perseverance the race marked out for us, fixing our eyes on Jesus, the pioneer and perfecter of faith. For the joy set before him he endured the cross, scorning its shame, and sat down at the right hand of the throne of God.

HEBREWS 12:1–2 NIV

No runner enters a race to lose. He sees himself crossing the finish line near the top of the pack. All marathon runners set out to finish well. Otherwise, why bother?

God wants you to finish well in every area of your life. You might not start off on the best footing, but you really can finish well by making good choices along the way.

Your thought life is very much like a marathon. This battle to clean up your thoughts won't be won in an instant. You're in this for the duration, and you have to go the distance, one errant thought at a time. But if you don't give up, if you strive every day to keep your thoughts and heart in alignment with the Word of God, you'll finish the race stronger than ever before.

I want to be a person who finishes well, Lord. Give me the tenacity to keep going even when I don't feel like it. Amen.

PRAYER JAR INSPIRATION:

God wants me to finish well.

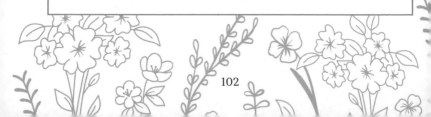

LETTING GO:
CODEPENDENT HEALING

Codependency is a psychological condition or relationship in which a person with low self-esteem or a desire for approval has an unhealthy attachment to an often controlling or manipulative person. Codependency can become a behavioral pattern where you become overly reliant on another person to meet your emotional needs. It's characterized by overindulging others to gain approval and validation—often at the sacrifice of your own well-being.

Children are dependent on their parents for physical and emotional needs. However, if the child is abused and gets blamed for abuse that's inflicted on them, they begin to believe the pain they have suffered is somehow their fault.

Codependent relationships get progressively worse over time, as the codependent person loses their sense of self, always trying to meet the other person's needs. Codependency can exist between friends as well as family members.

To break free from codependency and have a healthy relationship, the connection between two people needs to be mutual. Both parties need to care for each other and be willing to listen to the other. Breaking that dependency can be a challenge, and sometimes professional counseling is needed.

Christians should always be dependent on God. He is our helper in all things: "But the Helper, the Holy Spirit, whom the Father will send in My name, He will teach you all things, and bring to your remembrance all things that I said to you" (John 14:26 NKJV).

MUDDY WATERS

If the godly give in to the wicked, it's like
polluting a fountain or muddying a spring.
PROVERBS 25:26 NLT

Have you ever been in a codependent relationship? Such relationships can be tricky to navigate, for sure. Things can get very complicated when the other person emotionally manipulates you or tries to make you feel guilty for things you're not really guilty of.

Sometimes the Lord allows these relationships to remain, but from a greater distance. Other times He calls you to break off the relationship—for your own sanity and for the good of the person who has become too dependent on you.

You weren't created to carry another person's load. That's not to say you don't care and don't pray. Of course you do both of those things. But you know when things are out of balance, and that's not healthy for either of you.

If you're in a tricky relationship that needs healing, seek the Lord. Get His opinion. (It's the one that matters most, after all.) But do your best to stay out of muddy waters!

I won't muddy the waters by giving in to the nagging of
someone who wants me to carry their load, Lord. Amen.

PRAYER JAR INSPIRATION:

I will seek the Lord in all my relationships—
especially those that are tricky to navigate.

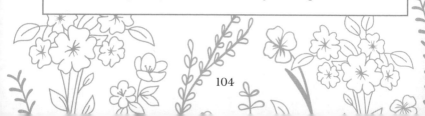

DRAINED DRY

For am I now seeking the approval of man, or of God?
Or am I trying to please man? If I were still trying to
please man, I would not be a servant of Christ.

GALATIANS 1:10 ESV

Codependent relationships always come with strings attached. Guilt attached. Fear attached.

When you're intrinsically linked to a person who is draining you dry, you'll never be able to do enough for them.

They will consume you, robbing you of other (healthier) relationships and causing you to doubt yourself in a thousand different ways.

It's time to take a giant step backward from codependent relationships. God wants you to be healthy, and that starts with taking care of yourself. (If you're too busy tending to the ever-present needs of a friend or loved one, you'll overlook your own needs. The enemy knows this and is counting on it!)

Ask God to relieve you of the guilt associated with taking a step back from the needy one. He will provide what that person needs and even knows who best to send to accomplish His will in his/her life. So rest easy. Leave the needy one in God's capable hands.

It's going to take courage to step back, Lord.
I'll need Your help with this. Amen.

PRAYER JAR INSPIRATION:

I'm no good to anyone when I'm drained dry. With God's help, I'll take a step back and reevaluate my own needs.

I CAN BE A GOD PLEASER

*But just as we have been approved by God to be
entrusted with the gospel, so we speak, not to
please man, but to please God who tests our hearts.*

1 Thessalonians 2:4 esv

She needs you. She *really, really* needs you. Or so it appears. Otherwise, why would she keep knocking at your door, flattering you for your ability to make her feel better?

So you keep giving. And giving. And giving. Your time. Your attention. Your advice. Your money. Your strategies. You give to the detriment of other relationships, and before long people are starting to notice. You've become her 911 call at all times of the day and night.

And now you're starting to wonder if you've given too much. This person seems to be joined at the hip, and you're getting nervous.

This is how codependent relationships transpire. They can slowly escalate over time, much like the frog in the pot of water, slowly coming to a boil and not even realizing it. You might be ready to ease away from the relationship, and that's probably a good thing. But you're not sure how. It's time to go to God and ask for very clear directions so that you make things better, not worse. He has a plan—for you and for your needy friend.

I will trust You, Lord, not myself. Amen.

PRAYER JAR INSPIRATION:

When I need help, God will always provide
clear direction for my relationships.

STUCK

It is for freedom that Christ has set us free. Stand firm, then,
and do not let yourselves be burdened again by a yoke of slavery.

GALATIANS 5:1 NIV

Have you ever watched an old movie where one of the characters got stuck in quicksand?

The physical act of being stuck in quicksand is a good analogy for what your life can be like when you're in a codependent relationship. You feel stuck. It feels like there is no way to break free from the tough position you find yourself in. And you wonder if you ever will.

So you convince yourself that the relationship isn't that bad. You say things like, "Well, he really needs me and it's good to be needed."

Is it? . . .

Here are a few questions to ask yourself:

Do I take better care of others than I take care of myself?

Do I worry more about the reactions of my loved one than my own feelings?

Do I feel stuck in this relationship?

Do I often feel bad about myself (as if I'm not doing enough)?

God always intended for us to live in relationships, but to join yourself to an individual who zaps you of your strength, one who pulls you into the quicksand? That was never part of His plan.

I'm stuck, Lord! I don't see a way out of this broken
relationship. Pull me from the quicksand, I pray. Amen.

PRAYER JAR INSPIRATION

When I choose to stand firm, I can
avoid getting stuck in quicksand.

ONLY ONE SAVIOR

*"From this man's descendants God has brought to
Israel the Savior Jesus, as he promised."*

ACTS 13:23 NIV

Codependent people can't seem to function on their own. They see you as a savior figure, someone who will sweep in and save the day when they end up in a jam. And let's face it: codependent people always end up in a jam.

The problem is, you're no savior. (You know it's true!) Despite your best attempts, you simply don't have what it takes to save another human being. From anger. From alcohol. From drugs. From pain.

Only Jesus can save. But He won't intervene in tough situations if you're standing in the way, playing His role in the story. Healing will never come to that other person if you've given yourself the lead role.

Move yourself to a secondary character part and let Jesus have His rightful place. When you do that, healing will come—to the other person and even to you. (You're pretty weary with this role, after all!)

*I'm tired of playing the role of savior, Jesus. It's not a role I was
ever meant to play. I hand the reins back to You today. Amen.*

PRAYER JAR INSPIRATION:
There's only one Savior—JESUS!

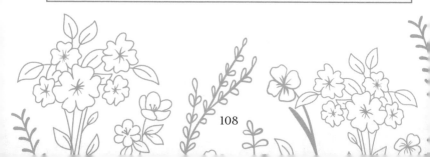

GIVE-AND-TAKE

The fear of man lays a snare, but whoever trusts in the LORD is safe.

PROVERBS 29:25 ESV

In many relationships, there's a taker and a giver. Attachments are formed that can turn unhealthy in a hurry, especially if the emotional and physical needs of one zap the other. Can you relate?

Maybe you've been in more than one friendship or romantic relationship where you found yourself on the "giver" side, rarely receiving anything in return. Those codependent relationships are draining, and they're wholly unfair. If one person always takes, expecting the other to give, how does that leave any room for God to work?

There's no room for healing in situations like that. The Lord can move only if you stop fixing the problem for the other person. It's time to rediscover boundaries. They can protect you from overgiving.

Or overtaking. If you've been the one zapping your friend or spouse, it's time to give them a break. Let God do what only God can do. He wants to bring healing.

It's been all give and no take in some of these
relationships, Jesus. Help me find balance. Amen.

PRAYER JAR INSPIRATION:

I will make room in my relationships
to let God do what only He can do.

SHOW *CO*- THE DOOR

*On the contrary, we speak as those approved by God
to be entrusted with the gospel. We are not trying to
please people but God, who tests our hearts.*

1 Thessalonians 2:4 niv

Co- is a funny little prefix. You see it in words like cohabitate, coexist, and so on. Usually *co-* attempts to bring people together. But sometimes this naughty little prefix goes a bit too far.

To codepend on someone means you can't function on your own. And, while it's great to live in community, God never intended for you not to be able to do most of life's most basic things on your own.

Co- tries to convince the dependent one that she can't possibly survive without the other's help. It whispers, "You're not enough." Or even, "God in you isn't enough."

But in Christ, you are enough. You don't need to place all your dependence on another human being when the Creator of the universe stands ready to intervene on your behalf with just a word.

Is it time to show *co-* the door? Perhaps. If you're in a relationship that tugs too hard on another, it might just be time to step back a few feet and try to tackle some challenges on your own. With God's help, you can. With God's help, you *will*!

*I need to learn boundaries and healthy relationships.
Release me from codependency, Lord, I pray. Amen.*

> ## PRAYER JAR INSPIRATION:
> *With God's help. . .I can!*

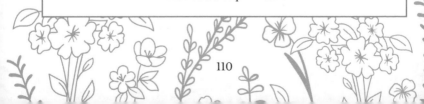

ABUSE

The Lord is a stronghold for the oppressed,
a stronghold in times of trouble.

PSALM 9:9 ESV

A codependent person gets his or her needs met through others, often those he (or she) has manipulated. This is both selfish and destructive.

When the term *codependent* was coined, it was a description of people who were bound to one another in an addictive relationship (like drugs or alcohol). These days, though, codependent relationships can be twisted and wound around all sorts of other things. And things get even trickier when one of the people in that relationship is abusive. There are destructive patterns seen in these highly volatile relationships that are hard to face and equally difficult to address.

If you find yourself in an abusive relationship today, do everything you can to get help. Pray for courage. Pray for strength. Confide in someone you trust. Trust the words in today's verse: *The Lord is a stronghold for the oppressed, a stronghold in times of trouble.*

God in you is greater than the person who has been hurting you. Your Creator is big enough, strong enough, and loving enough to rescue you—even from the most hurtful place. Hard as it might be, lean on Him to pull you from this situation, once and for all.

Thank You for being my stronghold, Jesus! Amen.

PRAYER JAR INSPIRATION:

God can—and *will*—set me free from harmful relationships.

WHO CARES WHAT THEY THINK?

Fearing people is a dangerous trap,
*but trusting the L*ORD *means safety.*
PROVERBS 29:25 NLT

One very telling aspect of codependency is the fear of man. You enter a relationship hoping it will be a two-way street, but when things go sideways you sometimes have trouble escaping because you're so afraid of what the other person will think. Or do.

The Bible refers to this as the fear of man, and Proverbs 29:25 shows us how God feels about that. The fear of man is a trap. Nothing good can come out of worrying endlessly about how others feel about your choices, your decisions, your beliefs, or your actions.

Instead of fretting over what others think, it's time to turn your attention back to Jesus. Care more about what He thinks. Your relationship with Christ is codependent in a completely different direction (a good direction). There's give-and-take from both of you, but He's definitely the one giving, giving, giving. . .more than He's taking!

Want to be healed from poor relationships? Focus on the one who matters most.

My relationship with You is the most important one in my life, Jesus.
I won't fret over what others think, only what You think. Amen.

PRAYER JAR INSPIRATION:

What's the most important relationship in my life?

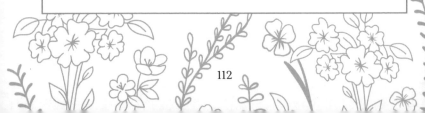

EQUAL WEIGHT

Carry each other's burdens, and in this
way you will fulfill the law of Christ.

GALATIANS 6:2 NIV

Perhaps you read all these devotions about codependency and think,
Now, wait a minute! Aren't we supposed to bear one another's burdens?
Isn't that the way Christians are supposed to live, holding up the arms of
the weaker ones?

Absolutely! That's definitely a specific call for believers, to carry
one another's burdens. But think about it like this: if you went on
a journey across the desert with two donkeys and one was loaded
down with all of the luggage but the other was bare backed, which
one would arrive in better shape?

Codependency doesn't share equally. It throws all the luggage onto
the shoulders of one friend—and the other walks freely. God never
intended us to live this way. We're to be equally yoked with fellow
believers so that we can carry one another's burdens, yes, but also so
that we can be a joy and encouragement to one another. That's hard
to do when you're completely weighed down. A healed relationship
is a balanced relationship.

I don't mind carrying burdens for others, Lord.
You've created me to do so. Heal my weak relationships
so that the burden is equally shared. Amen.

PRAYER JAR INSPIRATION:

I can keep my relationships in balance with God's help.

WELL, THAT DEPENDS

The fear of the Lord is the beginning of wisdom; all who follow his precepts have good understanding. To him belongs eternal praise.

PSALM 111:10 NIV

Have you ever been asked a question, perhaps something like: "Can you babysit the grandkids next Saturday?" And you respond with the words, "Well, that depends. Let me check my calendar to make sure I haven't already committed to something."

When one thing "depends" on another, outcomes are affected. You can't watch the grandkids if you've already promised to work at the homeless shelter that same day. And your daughter understands. (Or at least, she should!)

Life is filled with situations that depend on other situations. This is another reason why you can't allow yourself to get hung up in codependent relationships. You're already juggling enough. Situations are already getting pushed aside, one thing for the other, as it is.

If you take on someone else's stuff, you'll find yourself saying no to the grandkids. And that getaway with your best friend. And other things that could potentially be good for you.

When you're consumed with the wrong things, you won't have time to say yes to the good things. So, the next time that codependent friend says, "I need you to do XYZ for me," be firm and say, "Nope. Sorry. Can't." Then leave it at that.

Lord, thank You for the wisdom to know what to do in each situation. Amen.

PRAYER JAR INSPIRATION:
God will help me know when it's best to say yes. . .and no.

TAKING OUT THE TRASH

But let each one test his own work, and then his reason to
boast will be in himself alone and not in his neighbor.

GALATIANS 6:4 ESV

If you live in a residential neighborhood, you probably have trash pickup at least once a week, maybe two days per week, depending. And you pay for it—either directly, or through your utility bill or homeowner's fees.

Now imagine you had a neighbor who refused to pay his bill. So, he asked if he could use your trashcan to place his garbage. Out of the goodness of your heart, you agreed, but only for a brief period. But, weeks went by. Then months. And before long, your curb was covered in an overabundance of trash—from both houses. It wouldn't take long for the trash company to figure out what you were both up to, would it?

When you enter an elongated codependent relationship, you're offering to haul your friend's trash *and* pay for pickup. And the price can get very, very high. Once you've said yes to a person like this, wriggling out of it can be excruciating. (Hard lesson learned, for sure!) It's hard to say to a person, "Deal with your own trash," but sometimes those are the most loving words you can offer.

I need to heal from this desire to be all things to all
people, Jesus, but I will need Your help. Amen.

PRAYER JAR INSPIRATION:

I am not responsible for someone else's trash.

TEACH THEM TO WORK

All hard work brings a profit, but mere talk leads only to poverty.

PROVERBS 14:23 NIV

Imagine you're on a boat with your young son, teaching him to fish. He has a fish on the end of the line, and you're tempted to jump in, grab the pole, and reel it in for him.

But you don't. You stand close by (ready to intervene, if necessary), and explain, step by step, what he should do to reel this one in by himself.

And he does! He brings that fish onto the boat, and you all celebrate together.

This might seem like a silly illustration, but this is often what we do. We see a child (or a friend or loved one) struggling, and we immediately grab the pole. We take charge.

The problem with this method is that the person never learns how to reel that fish in on his own. And over time, he will become more and more dependent on you to keep him fed.

It's good to help. It's not good to take over completely.

Who's in the boat with you today? Which rod have you been clutching? Maybe it's time to pass it back to the real fisherman today.

This relationship can be healed if I let go of the pole,
Lord, but I'm going to need Your help. Amen.

PRAYER JAR INSPIRATION

I can let go of the pole so someone else can learn to fish for himself.

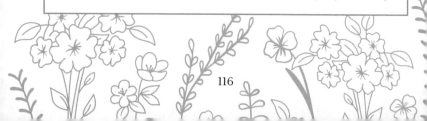

AM I THE NEEDY ONE?

*Do all you can to live a peaceful life. Take care of your own
business, and do your own work as we have already told you.
If you do, then people who are not believers will respect you,
and you will not have to depend on others for what you need.*

1 Thessalonians 4:11–12 ncv

Perhaps you're the one who's always tugging at others to help you.
You've convinced yourself you can't possibly make it on your own, so
you cling tight to the ones who offer the most moral support. This is
good. . .to a point.

If your neediness surpasses what's normal and healthy, your friend(s)
might be ready to pull away. And let's face it: it's not healthy for you
either. God wants you to learn to stand, not on your own two feet,
but with your hand firmly clasped in His. If you're too dependent on
your friends or family, you're probably not as dependent on Him as
you should be.

Today, decide to be healed from whatever it is that has held you
bound to people who are currently playing a God-like role in your
life. These folks aren't your savior. There's only one, and He already
paid the ultimate price so that you could live in total freedom. Today
is the day you can finally take steps in that direction by admitting
your need to Him.

*With Your help, I don't have to become dependent on others,
Lord. Please guard my heart and give me wisdom. Amen.*

PRAYER JAR INSPIRATION:

Jesus is my only Savior.

WAYMAKER

No temptation has overtaken you that is not common to man.
God is faithful, and he will not let you be tempted beyond
your ability, but with the temptation he will also provide
the way of escape, that you may be able to endure it.

1 CORINTHIANS 10:13 ESV

The Bible tells us that God makes a way where there seems to be no way. This was certainly true of the Israelites as they made the journey out of Egypt (bondage) into the promised land. They faced all sorts of obstacles along the way, including the ultimate one as the Egyptian army chased them into the Red Sea; but God miraculously parted the waters, and they came through on dry land. The Egyptians weren't so fortunate.

God provides for His own. He makes a way, even in seemingly impossible situations. If you've been feeling trapped, if you think there's no way out of your circumstances, look to the waymaker. If He did it for Moses, Aaron, and thousands of others, He will certainly do it for you.

He made a way for Paul and Silas out of a prison cell.

He made a way for the woman with the issue of blood.

He made a way for the thief on the cross.

And He will make a way for you too.

I can't depend on others to save me, Jesus, but I know that
You already have! May I always put my trust in You. Amen.

PRAYER JAR INSPIRATION:

Jesus is the waymaker.

A BALANCED WALK

*So I say, walk by the Spirit, and you
will not gratify the desires of the flesh.*

GALATIANS 5:16 NIV

There are many biblical references to oxen. Farmers would yoke them together to get tasks done. Why? Because two are stronger than one when they are in lockstep with each other.

If you've been involved in a codependent relationship or two, it's possible you fear all relationships. But this doesn't have to be the case. You can still be yoked to your godly friends in a healthy way.

A proper "yoking" is one in which everyone carries equal weight and does equal work. One in which you have each other's back. One in which the side-by-side journey is fair and balanced.

Don't be afraid to give your heart to a friend, even if you've been burned in the past. But prayerfully move into each relationship as God leads and watch as He shows you how to enjoy balanced and healthy friendships His way.

*I trust You to bring the right people my way, Lord.
I need good friends who won't let me down. Amen.*

PRAYER JAR INSPIRATION:

I will prayerfully enter all my relationships.

FIXING THE BROKEN THINGS

My son, be attentive to my words; incline your ear to my sayings.
Let them not escape from your sight; keep them within your heart.
For they are life to those who find them, and healing to all their flesh.
PROVERBS 4:20–22 ESV

There's your way, and then there's God's way. If you're like most, your way is the fast-track. You just want to deal with things, put them behind you, and move on. God's way can be a bit more intense. He wants you to deal with the broken things on the sidewalk behind you. (Hey, if you leave the broken bicycle on the pathway, someone else is sure to trip. It's not helping anyone to leave broken things exposed.)

God wants to fix the bike, not just drag it off the sidewalk. And when that bike represents a broken friendship, He wants to repair it for several reasons: the longer you leave that broken relationship out in the open, the more it affects your loved ones. Other friends get caught up in the fray. Your family suffers when you're hyper-focused on the one who hurt you.

So, when you're able, take the time to fix those broken relationships. Not all are meant to be, but the ones that are could potentially last for a lifetime.

I'll admit, it's easier not to fix broken things,
Lord. But I'll do it Your way! Amen.

PRAYER JAR INSPIRATION:

God's way is the healing way.

120

HEALING
FROM UNEXPECTED TRAUMA

People who deal with trauma and turn to God's Word fare better than those who don't. Traumatized people who frequently read the Bible are happier with where they are in the healing process and are more likely to experience relief than those who rarely open their Bibles.

While reading Scripture, people encounter Jesus Christ, the ultimate healer. He brings us hope, the key factor in the healing process.

We live in a broken world where bad things can happen, even to Christians. Despite the traumatic events, we can hope in Jesus Christ, knowing He has overcome our pain and trauma and can heal us of emotional hurt. God promises freedom from the trauma and hurt we may face. Though there is sorrow and grieving today, God brings mercies in the morning, fresh and renewed. He brings healing, not just to the physical body, but to the mind and soul. Jesus told His disciples that in this world, we will face trials: "These things I have spoken to you, that in Me you may have peace. In the world you will have tribulation; but be of good cheer, I have overcome the world" (John 16:33 NKJV).

A deep faith, nourished by scripture, gives us both internal and external resources that give hope and bring healing.

"He shall cover you with His feathers, and under His wings you shall take refuge; His truth shall be your shield and buckler" (Psalm 91:4 NKJV).

OUT OF THE RUBBLE

Then I said to them, "You see the trouble we are in: Jerusalem lies in ruins, and its gates have been burned with fire. Come, let us rebuild the wall of Jerusalem, and we will no longer be in disgrace."

NEHEMIAH 2:17 NIV

You never saw it coming. The tragedy hit from out of nowhere, almost wrecking you. Now you're standing in the rubble, looking at the shattered remains of what used to be, and wondering how to move forward from here. Is God going to miraculously glue those pieces back together and make life normal again?

This might be a good time to do a deep dive into the story of Nehemiah. He came back to Jerusalem to discover his beloved hometown in ruins. The walls were torn down and the city was reduced to rubble. For a while, all he could do was weep.

Then Nehemiah got busy, concocting a plan. In his mind's eye, he saw those walls rising again. And this man of God rose to the task, gathered the troops, and began the arduous process of rebuilding.

That's what it's going to take in your life too. After tragedy you might not feel like being tenacious, but with God's help you really can see your proverbial city rebuilt. It will take work. It will take courage. But you can heal, even after the most traumatizing event imaginable.

Lord, the walls of my life have crumbled, but I'm trusting You with the rebuilding process! Heal me, I pray.

PRAYER JAR INSPIRATION:

No matter how massive the pile of rubble, God is bigger still.

I LIFT MY EYES

I lift up my eyes to the hills. From where does my help come?
My help comes from the LORD, who made heaven and earth.
PSALM 121:1–2 ESV

An unexpected car accident. A cancer diagnosis. A divorce you never saw coming. These shockers are enough to send you reeling, careening down a cliff. And when you're in that fragile state, it's hard to make solid decisions.

If you're like most people, you barrel through the crises, smiling bravely and thinking, *I just need to get through this.* But that's not true. "Getting through it" isn't enough. You'll need time to deal with the pain. The grief. The trauma. You'll need plenty of rest on the other side of the chaos to heal your heart, your mind, and your soul.

But you're not inclined to think like that. So you plow forward, doing all the things you know to do, then dive right back into your work. It's a lovely distraction from the pain, right?

Wrong. God wants you to stop. To lift your head and your heart to search for Him. You can't fix this problem on your own, but He can. So lift your eyes to the hills. Your help comes from the Lord.

I won't look to myself for answers, especially during a hard
recovery, Lord. I will look only to You, my healer. Amen.

PRAYER JAR INSPIRATION:

I can lift my eyes from my circumstances and up to Jesus today!

FROZEN

I sought the Lord, and he answered me;
he delivered me from all my fears.

PSALM 34:4 NIV

In the deep winter, life slows down. Things freeze over. If you live in a place where you face particularly harsh winters, it's likely you face a lot of snow and ice days, where you're stuck at home, unable to go anywhere.

Those "frozen in" days are like what you go through after a period of shock. When startling (and deeply disturbing) things happen, it's as if you're locked down. Frozen. You couldn't function even if you wanted to.

During those frozen seasons, it's hard to envision springtime coming. But it will. The ice will melt. The situation will change. You will see the sun again. You will function properly again.

But in the meantime, allow God to hover close. He's with you, even in the dead of winter. If you seek Him, you will surely find Him, even in the middle of the trauma. And when you do, your worries and fears will begin to thaw in a way that could only be described as supernatural.

I need supernatural intervention, Lord!
I'm tired of living in frozen spaces! Amen.

PRAYER JAR INSPIRATION:

What areas of my life need thawing today?

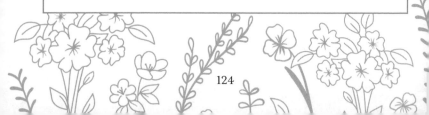

THE GOOD FIGHT

Fight the good fight of the faith. Take hold of the eternal life to which you were called and about which you made the good confession in the presence of many witnesses.

1 TIMOTHY 6:12 ESV

A fighter in the ring will get punched. He does his best to avoid it, ducking and turning, but he takes a lot of unexpected hits. Still, he has the knowledge in the back of his head that it's likely he will go down in the ring instead of coming out a victor. (Not every fighter wins every round, after all.)

Now think about your life. You're a lot like the fighter in the ring. But you forget that sometimes hard hits are to be expected. They catch you off guard. You don't have a strong defense. And then you find yourself on the floor of the ring, bloodied and wondering how you got there.

Life will knock you down from time to time. But a good fighter gets back up again. He lives to fight another day. You can have that mentality too. Don't let the hard knocks keep you on the floor. That's what your opponent wants. Rise, get healed, and get back in the ring.

I want to keep on going, Lord, even after the hard hits. Heal me so that I can keep moving forward, I pray. Amen.

PRAYER JAR INSPIRATION:

After a hard hit, I will trust God for healing so I can get back in the ring.

ROUGH SEASONS

*For though we live in the world, we do not wage war as the
world does. The weapons we fight with are not the weapons
of the world. On the contrary, they have divine power to
demolish strongholds. We demolish arguments and every
pretension that sets itself up against the knowledge of God,
and we take captive every thought to make it obedient to Christ.*

2 CORINTHIANS 10:3–5 NIV

When the human body goes into shock, multiple things happen: you
begin to shake uncontrollably, your ability to think clearly dissipates,
and tears often come. Many times you can't think clearly to know what
to do, so you must depend on others to guide you. (This is especially
true if you've been injured in an accident or have physical trauma.)

This isn't the time to beat yourself up for not being able to fix the
situation. You have to give yourself grace throughout the crises that
life throws your way.

Problems will come. The Bible doesn't say believers are immune.
But even in the thick of things, you can still feel the presence of God
and recognize that He is with you. He will never leave you or forsake
you—no matter how low things go.

And remember, even in the roughest of seasons, you've been given
weapons to use for warfare. And those weapons have divine, God-
breathed power to demolish strongholds!

*You've given me powerful weapons, Lord. Now give me clarity
of mind to know how and when to use them. Amen.*

PRAYER JAR INSPIRATION:

God is with me in every crisis.

RECOVERING FROM TRAUMA

Tell everyone who is discouraged, "Be strong and don't be afraid!
God is coming to your rescue, coming to punish your enemies."

ISAIAH 35:4 GNT

Trauma can be physical, psychological, or emotional. No doubt you've experienced various traumas through the years in all three areas. If you think about it, trauma is really a reaction (or a response) to what has happened. It seems to happen automatically.

The lingering effects of trauma can affect every area of your life. After a terrible car crash, you might be afraid to get in a vehicle again. After your child comes close to drowning, you might try to keep him from ever swimming again.

We do all sorts of things to avoid future traumas because we know how devastating they can be.

That said, Jesus doesn't want you to live in fear. Part of the reason He heals you from trauma is so you can move forward into the future without being locked up in dread. If you're still holding tightly to anguish over an old trauma, today is a good day to let it go. Why? So it doesn't spill over into tomorrow.

I can only get past this with Your help, Jesus. Amen.

PRAYER JAR INSPIRATION:

I will ask God to provide the courage
I need as I heal from my trauma.

BETTER TOGETHER

*Two people are better off than one, for they can help each other
succeed. If one person falls, the other can reach out and help. But
someone who falls alone is in real trouble. Likewise, two people
lying close together can keep each other warm. But how can one
be warm alone? A person standing alone can be attacked and
defeated, but two can stand back-to-back and conquer. Three
are even better, for a triple-braided cord is not easily broken.*

ECCLESIASTES 4:9–12 NLT

Have you ever wondered why fish swim in schools? There are a host
of reasons why they stick together; here are two. First, they are better
protected against predators when they remain together. Second, they
receive social benefits from being in a school. Their interactions with
one another form behavior patterns and help them develop socially.

It's the same with you. God designed you to live in community.
This is especially critical when you're going through a crisis. It's almost
impossible for the lone fish to survive the crisis. But when he's surrounded by his brothers and sisters, fully engulfed in that social circle
of the protective school, his chances go way up.

One of the ways God wants you to heal from crises is by drawing
close to those He's placed in your proverbial school. They're there,
arms outstretched, waiting to walk you through this. Don't run from
them. Instead, draw close.

Thank You, Lord, for sending people I can share life with. Amen.

PRAYER JAR INSPIRATION:

We really are better together.

BE PREPARED

Whoever works his land will have plenty of bread,
but he who follows worthless pursuits lacks sense.

PROVERBS 12:11 ESV

Have you heard of the prepper movement? These people are prepared for anything—incoming storms, famine, earthquakes—pretty much anything you could name. They stock their pantries with goods to last for weeks (or even months or years). They have generators, water, and dehydrated food products. They're ready. They have enough toilet paper to last into the next decade and fresh water to hydrate their families for months to come.

You could say these people live in a constant sense of expectation. There's always the feeling that something might be coming, and they want to be ready.

The problem with unexpected crises is that you're never prepared for those. There's no prepper kit for a cancer diagnosis or an automobile accident that takes the life of your child. No storage shed in the world is large enough to hold the grief when your spouse walks out to marry someone else or when your boss says, "Sorry, but we have to let you go." You're stuck. . .unprepared.

But God is never unprepared. You might say He's the greatest prepper of all time. He has everything you need, and He is (literally) as close as your next breath. So, don't panic. Reach out to the one who not only saw your crisis coming but has already made provision for it.

Thank You for being the best prepper of all time, Lord! Amen.

PRAYER JAR INSPIRATION:

God is always prepared.

HE HAS YOU COVERED

He will cover you with his feathers. He will shelter you with his wings.
His faithful promises are your armor and protection. Do not be
afraid of the terrors of the night, nor the arrow that flies in the day.

PSALM 91:4–5 NLT

Do you know someone who works as an emergency responder? It would take a very special kind of person to be able to roll up on a horrific accident and jump into action to save lives. Most of us would freeze up, unsure of what to do. But the EMS worker is trained for an event such as this.

The same is true with doctors and nurses who work in the ER. Not just anyone could do that kind of work, especially the more squeamish or doubtful among us. You need someone who can see beyond the pain and straight to the solution.

When you've been through a trauma, it's good to surround yourself with spiritual EMS workers. You need friends and companions alongside you who won't panic. It's important to locate the ones who are skilled at stopping gaping wounds.

God has you covered—whether He chooses to intervene supernaturally or send friends or loved ones with just the right skills to help you through the trauma you're facing. You might see trauma, but they see solutions.

Thank You for the solution seekers in my life, Lord! I'm so
grateful for friends who know what to do. Amen.

PRAYER JAR INSPIRATION:

God has me covered.

PILED ON

In all of this, Job did not sin by blaming God.

JOB 1:22 NLT

Have you ever read the book of Job? Poor guy was hard hit by disaster. He started out with an ideal life—great family, great home, great income, great friends, great health.

By the time his story ended, he'd lost nearly everything. Like dominoes, it all came tumbling down. And all along the way, Job had the option of turning his back on God (of blaming Him, even) but he managed to hold tight to his faith.

When the dominoes are tumbling like that, it's natural to despair and to point fingers. After all, if God loved you, why would He allow all of this? Couldn't He stop it if He truly cared?

These challenges provide the perfect opportunity for God's intense love for you to shine through, even in the deepest valley. He doesn't plan to ever leave you or forsake you, so don't turn your back on Him either! You need Him in the valley. And on the mountaintop. And every place in between.

I won't point a finger at You, God. I'll keep trusting
even when nothing is going my way. Amen.

PRAYER JAR INSPIRATION:

Even when the dominoes tumble, if I trust God, I won't fall.

DECISIONS, DECISIONS

"Why can't you decide for yourselves what is right?"

LUKE 12:57 NLT

How do you heal from a broken heart or wounded spirit? Slowly. Carefully. Methodically.

Some people tend to rush through the process. It's not unusual to see a newly divorced person immediately jump into the dating scene or even marry a near stranger. They think this will bring healing, but it usually just heaps more problems on top of an already traumatized heart.

Making quick decisions when you haven't taken the time to heal can land you in precarious positions and not just relational decisions. Financial decisions are harder when your mind and heart are still twisted up in the pain of what you've been through. (A lot of people drown their sorrows at the mall, spending money they don't need to be spending.)

Take time to heal before you make life-altering decisions. No rash ones or you might just have to pay a price.

Help me choose wisely, Lord. I don't want to
make rash decisions I will later regret. Amen.

PRAYER JAR INSPIRATION:
Slow, careful, truth-filled decisions are always best.

FEAR OF REPEATS

Such love has no fear, because perfect love expels all fear.
If we are afraid, it is for fear of punishment, and this shows
that we have not fully experienced his perfect love.

1 JOHN 4:18 NLT

"It's going to happen again."

When you've been hard-hit with a trauma, sometimes you slip into fear mode, convincing yourself that the trauma is going to hit again. If, for instance, a burglar breaks into your home and steals some of your belongings, you might live in constant fear that he's coming back, even though the police now have him in their custody.

This reaction is completely normal post-trauma, and you're certainly not alone. But God doesn't want you to live in fear.

The enemy would love nothing more than to keep you bound up, waiting for the next shoe to drop. But most of the things we worry about don't actually come to pass (thank goodness)! So, don't give away hours of your life to fear of the unknown. Instead, acknowledge those fears. Be honest with God. Say, "I'm really scared this is going to happen again." Then allow Him to drive out that fear with His perfect love.

Thank You for the reminder that I don't have to live in fear, Lord. Amen.

PRAYER JAR INSPIRATION:

God's perfect love drives out fear.

SCARS

"He went to him and bandaged his wounds, pouring on oil and wine. Then he put the man on his own donkey, brought him to an inn and took care of him."

LUKE 10:34 NIV

When you cut your finger, a scar forms, sealing the broken places back together. And when you've been through personal (emotional, physical, or mental) trauma, scars form as well.

Sometimes scars are visible. People notice them and are reminded to ask how you're doing post-trauma.

But sometimes scars are hidden, buried deep in your thought life or your heart. People don't see them and don't think to ask how you're doing. So you hunker down even more, convinced no one sees or knows what you're going through.

The truth is, we all have scars. And they are nothing to be ashamed of. They are a sign (to you and others) that healing is taking place. So don't hide those scars. They're a reminder that God is already at work.

Thank You for the healing that is already taking place in my heart and mind, Lord. I'm not ashamed of these scars. They're a sign that You are working in my life.

PRAYER JAR INSPIRATION:

My scars are beautiful.

UNEXPECTED

Behold, God is my helper; the Lord is the upholder of my life.

PSALM 54:4 ESV

When you're expecting a baby, you have nine months to prepare yourself for the baby's arrival. Nine months to buy baby furniture. Nine months to figure out your work situation. Nine months to choose the baby's name.

God knew you would need time, and so He created a nine-month window to get everything done. And best of all, there's a sense of expectation that makes the journey even more fun.

Not everything can be planned out like that. Sometimes things hit unexpectedly. A job loss. The death of a loved one. A stock market crash. And you've had zero time to prepare. So, you go into it completely blinded. There's been no sense of expectation, no clue this would hit. Yet here you are.

Isn't it comforting to realize that God knew this was coming and has already seen what's ahead for you? He loves you very much and will always take care of you, so you have nothing to fear. No matter what comes—expected or unexpected—He has already made provision for it.

I can trust You with the unexpected, Lord. Amen.

PRAYER JAR INSPIRATION:

God is my helper, even in the unexpected.

SURVIVE. . .OR THRIVE?

"They will thrive like well-watered grass,
like willows by streams of running water."

Isaiah 44:4 GNT

Think of the people who've been through legitimate traumas: Holocaust survivors. Fire survivors. Abuse survivors. So many have been through the fire and lived to tell about it.

All these people have one very important word in common: *survivor*. It's a powerful word to define them, but there's another word even more powerful: *thriver*.

God doesn't just want you to survive life's tragedies, He longs for you to thrive on the opposite side of them. It might seem impossible now, but you really can grow and become more like Christ from the hard road you've walked. When you do that, you can turn survival into a life of thriving.

You've been shaped and formed into His image as you've gone through the fire. Now you're ready to minister to others with a sensitivity and power you never had before. Nothing can hold you back now.

I want to thrive—like willows by streams of running water, Lord. Thank You for bringing me out on the other side so I can do that. Amen.

PRAYER JAR INSPIRATION:

Because of Jesus, I'm thriving like well-watered grass.

BREAK THE CIRCUITS

*I know what it is to be in need, and I know what it is to have
plenty. I have learned the secret of being content in any and every
situation, whether well fed or hungry, whether living in plenty or
in want. I can do all this through him who gives me strength.*

PHILIPPIANS 4:12–13 NIV

When you face an unexpected trauma, it puts all your senses on alert.
Your poor nervous system is suddenly overloaded with the equivalent
of a power surge. And just like in a real storm, the aftereffects can
be hard. When a power surge takes place in your home, there's the
initial jolt that knocks everything offline. No more power. No more
cable. No more. . .anything.

And that's kind of how it is for your body post-surge, as well.

You can't think. You can't eat. You can't sleep. You can't. . .anything.
It's as if someone has flipped the switch and shut everything down.

In a storm, you wait for an employee of the power company to
climb that pole and fix the broken line. In your heart, you wait for the
ultimate power source, God Almighty, to restore power once again.

He will. It might take time before you can function properly again,
but He will restore you. In fact, your heavenly lineman has already
finished the job. He risked everything to see you healed and whole.

I can do all things through You, Jesus! Amen.

PRAYER JAR INSPIRATION:

A power surge doesn't have to cause a power outage.

THE TSUNAMI: WHEN THOSE FEELINGS RETURN

His anger lasts only a moment, his goodness for a lifetime.
Tears may flow in the night, but joy comes in the morning.

PSALM 30:5 GNT

If you've shut down after a trauma, the feelings will return. But when they do, look out!

Sometimes feelings come in like a flood. A tsunami, even. Anger often leads the way. You don't really know why you're so angry, and you can't seem to control it, but there it is, rearing its ugly head.

Why? Because anger is one of the many stages of grief. (And let's face it, the stages of grief don't play nice!) Anger can lead to outbursts you might regret later.

When this tsunami hits, it's common to gush all over anyone who happens to be in your path. (Pity the person who lands in front of you on the day when you're worked up!) And while it might seem uncontrollable, you will begin to see patterns of reactionary behaviors that can be controlled, at least to some extent.

So watch out for the tsunamis. Don't let them sweep you out to sea. And remember: the Bible says that God gets angry too. But His anger lasts only for a moment. His goodness lasts a lifetime.

When angry moments come, help me
keep them under control, Lord. Amen.

PRAYER JAR INSPIRATION:

I will not allow my emotions to rule me.

BROKEN DREAMS:
HEALING WHEN THINGS DON'T GO THE WAY YOU THOUGHT THEY WOULD

We all have those days when things don't seem to go our way and one or two small occurrences can ruin everything for us. If there is one thing circumstances teach us, it's that we aren't always in control of the things that happen around us. We're in control of very few things. That fact can sometimes scare us into a wave of anxiety or panic.

God reminds us that even when we aren't in control, there is nothing to worry about because He controls everything. Some days may not always go smoothly, but in the midst of chaos, God can make all things work together for our good if we put our trust in Him instead of trying to gain control when we're unable and in need of His help.

Here are a few scriptures to focus on when your day isn't going the way you had planned.

"Trust in the LORD with all your heart, and lean not on your own understanding; in all your ways acknowledge Him, and He shall direct your paths" (Proverbs 3:5–6 NKJV).

"The LORD will guide you continually, and satisfy your soul in drought, and strengthen your bones; you shall be like a watered garden, and like a spring of water, whose waters do not fail" (Isaiah 58:11 NKJV).

"I will instruct you and teach you in the way you should go; I will guide you with My eye" (Psalm 32:8 NKJV).

CHOOSE JOY

Always be joyful. Never stop praying.
Be thankful in all circumstances, for this is
God's will for you who belong to Christ Jesus.

1 Thessalonians 5:16–18 nlt

Can you imagine choosing not to heal? What if you looked at your broken arm and said, "Bones, I command you not to fuse back together!" That would be crazy, right?

It's equally strange that we go through seasons where we would rather wallow in our grief than pick up the pieces, get the healing we need, and move forward.

Maybe this is why the Bible says we are to "choose" joy. We must put it on like we would choose a blouse or a skirt. We choose joy even when we don't feel like it. (And let's face it: some days we really, *really* don't feel like it.)

Why? Because it's hard to heal when you're down in the dumps. It's difficult to mend a broken leg if you keep removing the cast. Joy brings life to the bones and health to the body. And ultimately, that's God's way!

So choose joy today. In doing so, you are saying, "I choose healing!"

It's hard to imagine always being joyful, but I will
do my best, Lord. Give me Your version of joy,
the kind that rises above circumstances. Amen.

PRAYER JAR INSPIRATION:

Today I choose joy!

I WON'T HEAL ON MY OWN

All the people tried to touch him, for power was
going out from him and healing them all.

LUKE 6:19 GNT

Inanimate objects don't heal on their own. A broken platter doesn't miraculously come together over time like a broken bone would. A busted radiator won't fix itself. It takes a skilled worker with just the right instruments to bring those things back together again.

You're not an inanimate object but there really are times when you say, "I just can't. I don't have it in me." Aren't you glad, in those times, that the master craftsman is nearby, ready to put the pieces back together again?

Look at today's verse. People clustered around Jesus because He gained a reputation as a healer. They knew just where to go for their healing. And when they got close enough for a touch, power went out of Him!

That same life-giving power still flows from Jesus today. So look to Him for whatever you need.

Thank You, Lord, for healing Your children! Amen.

PRAYER JAR INSPIRATION:
When I can't, God can.

WE ARE THE
DREAMERS OF DREAMS

In the beginning God created the heavens and the earth.

GENESIS 1:1 NLT

There's a fun line in the movie *Willy Wonka and the Chocolate Factory*, where Wonka says, "We are the music-makers. We are the dreamers of dreams." Maybe you can relate. Maybe you've always been a dreamer too. You've imagined amazing things for yourself. And maybe you're disappointed because they haven't come to pass yet.

Sure, you have amazing ideas. You're created in the image of the same God who created the heavens and the earth, after all! And you've worked hard to implement your ideas and bring them to fruition. But perhaps things didn't pan out and you're disappointed. Broken, even.

God created the Willy Wonkas of this world. He plants dreams and visions deep in the hearts of His children. Some of them are meant to blossom and grow. Others are meant to serve as stepping stones to other (bigger!) things.

No matter where you are, don't let the disappointment get to you. If your dream didn't come to pass, give it to Jesus. The timing. The outcome. All of it. And remember: He has big plans for you, probably even bigger than you have for yourself.

I will do my best not to get anxious when things don't happen according to my timeline, Lord. Amen.

PRAYER JAR INSPIRATION:

God made me to be a dreamer of dreams.

APPLES OF GOLD IN SETTINGS OF SILVER

Like apples of gold in settings of silver is a ruling rightly given. Like an earring of gold or an ornament of fine gold is the rebuke of a wise judge to a listening ear.

PROVERBS 25:11–12 NIV

A word in due season can go a long, long way in turning a person's situation around.

Do you have a friend or loved one who is struggling to find their way today? Speak words of life over them. Is someone grieving the loss of a job or a dream? Offer uplifting, hopeful words.

"Like apples of gold in settings of silver." What do you suppose that means? The ordinary becomes extraordinary with a few words of love poured on top. A child suddenly sees himself as special. An elderly friend is reminded of why she's amazing. A coworker's spirits are lifted as you share a pat on the back.

These might seem like small things, but they're not. If you could put a dollar value on encouraging words, the price would start at about a million dollars a word. That's how much they mean to the one on the receiving end.

So what's keeping you? Is a friend struggling? Drop some million-dollar words on her today!

I want to speak high-dollar words, Lord! Show me how to share positive, upbeat conversations with those who need them the most.

PRAYER JAR INSPIRATION:

Words matter.

REALISTIC DREAMS

*For when dreams increase and words grow many, there
is vanity; but God is the one you must fear.*

ECCLESIASTES 5:7 ESV

Some folks have their dreams squashed quickly, simply because they're not realistic. Not everyone becomes a millionaire overnight. Some people work for years and don't hit their goals.

Today, look at some of your dreams that didn't come true—the ones you've grieved over—and give them a realistic look. Were they doable or some sort of get-rich-quick scheme? (Hey, there's nothing wrong with earning good money, but instant success is an illusion, not a reality.)

Perhaps it's time to reframe those dreams. Give them a longer timeline. Look at them from a different angle. Pray that God will reveal a better way to accomplish what He has put in your heart to do.

And don't give in to despair when those dreams don't come true. Hindsight, as they say, is 20/20. Later you'll be glad that all your dreams didn't come true. Some could have led you down a dark road, away from God and from His people. In other words, thank Him for the dreams that didn't work out. They might have been a saving grace!

When my dreams are unrealistic, Lord, show me! (I can take it!) Amen.

PRAYER JAR INSPIRATION:

*Not all dreams need to come true, and that's okay.
God has something bigger—and better—in store for me.*

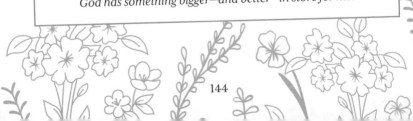

GOD AT THE CENTER

*"But when he, the Spirit of truth, comes, he will guide you into
all the truth. He will not speak on his own; he will speak only
what he hears, and he will tell you what is yet to come."*

JOHN 16:13 NIV

Is God at the center of your dreams? Maybe you have big ideas, big visions for the future. Great! But is He at the very center of them? Were these God-breathed ideas or things you came up with after watching an infomercial? (Hey, legit question!)

God dreams are most often bigger than yourself. They can seem impossible, even a little intimidating. But when God is in a thing, all things are possible!

Maybe you've had attainable dreams, things that should have come to pass but didn't. Why? Perhaps God wasn't in them. You can walk away from those situations feeling defeated and hopeless. And let's face it, asking God to enter your dream isn't exactly a strategy for success.

It needs to be the other way around. If you are healing from a broken heart over crushed dreams, ask God to show you His plans, His dreams, His strategies. He will, you know! He wants you to succeed. And when you give Him His rightful place—the very center of it all—you will!

*To keep You at the center, I have to invite Your Spirit to rule
and reign. I choose to do that today, Lord. Amen.*

PRAYER JAR INSPIRATION:

I will ask God to show me His dreams for my life.

IT'S NOT THE END OF THE ROAD

As you come to him, the living Stone—rejected by humans but chosen by God and precious to him—you also, like living stones, are being built into a spiritual house to be a holy priesthood, offering spiritual sacrifices acceptable to God through Jesus Christ.

1 PETER 2:4–5 NIV

Remember what it felt like as a teen to have a crush on a boy? Maybe you expressed your feelings, but then he rejected you. Ouch!

The pain of rejection is a terrible thing to deal with, especially when you pinned all your hopes on that person. Now, as an adult, you've probably experienced the same pain in a variety of ways. Maybe you pinned all of your hopes on a new job opportunity, and it didn't happen. Or maybe you felt sure you would have a child, only to have a pregnancy end in miscarriage. Broken dreams come in all sorts of ways.

It's never good to put all your hopes and dreams in one basket. Diversify! That way, when one road comes to an end, you have others to follow. But remember, God is there with you, traveling those broken roads. And He already sees into tomorrow and knows that great things are coming. So hang on! There's plenty of road ahead for you.

Thank You that broken dreams don't mean the end of the road, Jesus! Amen.

PRAYER JAR INSPIRATION:

It's not the end of the road for me!

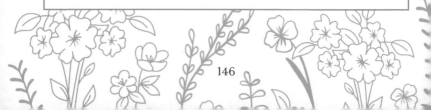

ONE DAY AT A TIME, SWEET JESUS

"So do not worry about tomorrow; it will have enough worries of its own. There is no need to add to the troubles each day brings."

MATTHEW 6:34 GNT

If you're like most people, you've prayed for God to heal your emotions (say, a broken heart after a failed relationship), and He's done so. You walked in freedom for a while. Then it all started up again. Something triggered a memory, and the memory triggered an emotional response. Before you knew it, tears were rolling, just like they used to.

There's a reason Jesus encouraged us to live one day at a time. Each day truly does have enough trouble of its own. And healing doesn't mean you'll never hurt again. It means you're not driven by the brokenness anymore. You're driving a different car, one with a better engine. You might still have a few breakdowns on the way to your destination, but you'll get there.

Don't beat yourself up if you don't have it all together right away. These things take time, after all. Just rest easy in the fact that your heart is safe in the hands of the healer, who loves you more than life itself.

I know this is a process, Jesus. I will trust You,
even on the tear-filled days. Amen.

PRAYER JAR INSPIRATION:

I can trust God even on the hard days.

OUR WONDERFUL CREATOR

"You are worthy, our Lord and God, to receive glory
and honor and power, for you created all things, and by
your will they were created and have their being."

REVELATION 4:11 NIV

The same creative God who made blowfish, giraffes, and Siamese kittens made you. He doesn't suffer from a lack of creativity! Neither do you, though you might not consider yourself the creative type. You are created in His image, after all.

When you have your heart set on something—say, a big dream—and it doesn't come to fruition, it's tempting just to give up. But that's not what a child of God does. (God never gives up, after all.) You're creative enough, and tenacious enough, to begin again, even after a big disappointment.

Things might not look the way you expected. God might not even use the same people you expected. But your creative God is nudging you today to say, "Hey, don't stop now! We have work to do."

You do, you know. So stop fretting over what didn't happen and start looking ahead to what could happen.

Thank You, my creative Father, for creating me in Your image!
Help me to keep going even when I don't feel like it!

PRAYER JAR INSPIRATION:

I'm a child of the Most High God, and I won't give up!

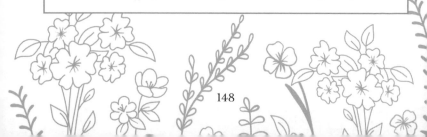

KINTSUGI

My sacrifice, O God, is a broken spirit; a broken
and contrite heart you, God, will not despise.

PSALM 51:17 NIV

In Japanese tradition, a broken plate or piece of pottery is put back together with liquid gold (known as gold joinery or *kintsugi*). In this process, liquid gold fills the cracks of a broken vessel, forming a lovely, finished product, even better than before.

No doubt you've been through some major breaks in your life. And you've done your best to mend and allow yourself to move forward. But you've still envisioned those cracks as something ugly—a negative testimony, as it were.

But they're not ugly at all!

Your master craftsman has used His own special version of gold, mending you and making you into a thing of beauty. So, as you look at where you've been—what you've been through—begin to see yourself as a beautiful work of art, pieced together by the master craftsman, with skillful artistry.

You have mended me into a thing of beauty, Lord, and I'm so grateful!

PRAYER JAR INSPIRATION:

Jesus is the ultimate mender!

THE END OF A THING

Better is the end of a thing than its beginning, and the
patient in spirit is better than the proud in spirit.

ECCLESIASTES 7:8 ESV

Have you ever played that game where you rewrite the endings of
fairy tales? It's interesting to twist up the stories. What if Cinderella
didn't end up with the prince? What if Snow White didn't eat the
poisoned apple? What if Rapunzel had short hair?

Not every real-life story ends the way you think it will. No doubt
you've been somewhat conditioned by fairy tales to think there's a
happily-ever-after, but reality often says otherwise. And the believer
isn't exempt from pain and heartache. (Blame Adam and Eve! God
created us to live in the bliss of Eden, and they blew it big-time!)

You don't get to write the ending of your story, but you can most
assuredly control the type of role you play in it. You can be a protag-
onist (working with God) or an antagonist (kicking and screaming,
fighting Him all the way). When things don't go your way, bow your
heart to the Creator of all and trust that no matter how tough the
battle, He's planning to fight it for you.

I'm trusting You to write my story, Lord! Amen.

PRAYER JAR INSPIRATION:

God is the very best story-teller!

GOD'S PLANS

May he give you the desire of your heart and
make all your plans succeed.

PSALM 20:4 NIV

God's plans for our lives don't always match our own. We move forward, confident we're following hard after Him, only to face disappointments.

Such was the case with Jesus' cousin John. John was the forerunner of Jesus, the one who led the way. Many believers came to faith because of the hard work this amazing man of God did. Unfortunately, all that good work landed him in prison—not a place he expected to be. In that low place, John began to question God's plans for him. He sent word to Jesus from inside his prison cell, asking, "Are you the Messiah, or should we look for another?" (Luke 7:20 paraphrased). Wow. Talk about falling to a low place.

No doubt you've never been to prison for your faith. But you've experienced disappointments. You had lofty dreams that didn't come through. And you've developed your own prison-cell doubts.

Jesus never got mad at John for questioning Him, and He isn't mad at you either. Disappointments come and acknowledging them isn't wrong. So whatever you're thinking or feeling today, don't be afraid to bring those questions straight to the throne of God, where the only answers lie.

Thank You for letting me bring my questions to You, Lord. Amen.

PRAYER JAR INSPIRATION:

I will not let disappointment conquer me.

ALMOST

But the plans of the Lord stand firm forever,
the purposes of his heart through all generations.

PSALM 33:11 NIV

Did you realize that Moses never actually made it to the promised land? Almost. . .but not quite.

Stephen, one of the early church leaders, wasn't able to meet his goal of reaching the world with the gospel message. He was stoned to death at a relatively young age.

Civil rights leader Martin Luther King Jr., who penned the "I Have a Dream" speech, didn't live to see his dream on this earth come true, not in his lifetime.

Many times God places dreams and visions in the hearts of people who don't get to see them all the way to the end. But before you cry out, "That's not fair!" understand that He places those same dreams in the hearts of hundreds, if not thousands, of other believers too.

Moses wasn't meant to lead his people all the way into the promised land, but Joshua was. Stephen didn't live to spread the gospel, but a rogue-turned-believer named Paul was. And Martin Luther King Jr. didn't live to see children overcome persecution, but many of his friends and companions continued to fight for their rights.

God always makes a way and always plants dreams in the hearts of men and women.

You always make a way, Lord. How grateful I am. Amen.

PRAYER JAR INSPIRATION:

God's purposes will stand.

FIXATED

Fixing our eyes on Jesus, the pioneer and perfecter of faith. For the joy set before him he endured the cross, scorning its shame, and sat down at the right hand of the throne of God.

HEBREWS 12:2 NIV

Have you ever been fixated on something? Maybe you had your eye on a particular model of car and made up your mind to get it at any cost. Or maybe you set your heart on that special someone, only to be disappointed in the end.

When we're fixated on something, it means our focus is so narrow we can't see past it. The house could be burning down around us, and we wouldn't notice when we're fixated.

The problem with twenty-first-century fixation is that we're usually not fixated on Jesus. More likely we're hyper-focused on stuff. Or our job. Or a relationship. Or a problem. We're staring so intently at it that we forget God is right next to us wishing He had our full attention.

Want to recover from the traumas that have plagued you? Take your eyes off whatever they're staring at and put them on Jesus, the author and finisher of your faith. He deserves every moment of your time and attention.

I will keep fixated on You, Jesus! Amen.

PRAYER JAR INSPIRATION:

Heavenly fixation is a good thing.

THE DREAMER

*[Joseph] had a dream, and when he told it to his brothers,
they hated him all the more. He said to them, "Listen to this
dream I had: We were binding sheaves of grain out in the field
when suddenly my sheaf rose and stood upright, while your
sheaves gathered around mine and bowed down to it."*

GENESIS 37:6–7 NIV

If you've read the story of Joseph, found in Genesis 37, you know that he was a big dreamer. He had (literal) dreams that one day his brothers would bow down to him. They weren't amused. So they took that dreamer and tossed him into a pit, then sold him into slavery to the Egyptians.

Not everyone is going to like hearing about your dreams, especially if they're "big" dreams. You'll have naysayers. You'll have those who are angry when you succeed. (Jealous much?) And you'll have the "I told you so" crowd when your dreams don't come to pass the way you hoped (or expected) they would.

Joseph didn't let the negativity get to him. In the end, his dream actually came to pass. He was eventually placed in charge of Pharaoh's palace in Egypt; and when his brothers came to Egypt in search of food, they did, indeed, end up bowing down to him.

Dreams will be broken. People will rub it in. But you can pick up the pieces and dare to dream again. Be a Joseph. Hang in there.

*Thank You for the God-sized dreams You've placed inside of me,
Lord! I won't give up when things don't go my way. Amen.*

PRAYER JAR INSPIRATION:

*I won't let the naysayers distract me from
the dreams God has planted in my heart.*

RECOVERING FROM
A CROOKED PATH

*Trust in the Lord with all your heart and lean not on
your own understanding; in all your ways submit to
him, and he will make your paths straight.*

PROVERBS 3:5–6 NIV

When dreams seem to be irretrievably broken, you can feel completely alone. No one else had the passion for that dream like you did. No one else feels the disappointment you feel. In fact, many don't even seem to notice how deeply you're grieving this loss.

But you're feeling it to the core. You're second-guessing yourself and wondering if maybe you were wrong to hope, wrong to dream.

Those dreams, if God-breathed, will only come according to His calendar. And you simply don't know His timeline. It could be He's protecting you from pain by not letting it happen yet. Only time will tell.

But in the meantime, be reminded: you are never alone. Never. Even when the path is brutally crooked, God is right there, holding you tight. If you're stuck, He's there. If you're moving forward, He's there.

He will never leave you or forsake you. Ever. You can still trust Him to make your path straight, no matter how crooked it has been.

*I'm weary from the broken, crooked paths, Lord. But I'm
trusting You to straighten the road ahead. Amen.*

PRAYER JAR INSPIRATION:

God can make my way straight.

IN THE NAME OF THE LORD ALMIGHTY

David answered, "You are coming against me with sword, spear, and javelin, but I come against you in the name of the LORD Almighty, the God of the Israelite armies, which you have defied."

1 SAMUEL 17:45 GNT

David, the shepherd boy, was on his way to the battlefield, not to fight, but to deliver food to the older, more capable warriors.

When he arrived, he saw that his people were squared off against a giant of a man—Goliath. Some say that Goliath was over nine feet tall. (Can you imagine a young boy facing such a man?)

Goliath stood at a distance, taunting and ridiculing the Jewish people, and David couldn't abide the vile words coming from the Philistine's mouth. So he flew into action, ready to take him down. He didn't have dreams of being a giant-killer, but in the moment, God gave him the courage and tenacity to get the job done. With a slingshot and a stone, he took that giant down.

You might not dream of being a giant-killer either. But God has already placed inside of you the courage to do remarkable things when the situation calls for it. So don't worry about the giants in your path. The Lord is already making a way.

In Your name, I can take down my enemies, Lord! Amen.

PRAYER JAR INSPIRATION:

The name of Jesus is more powerful than anything I will ever face.

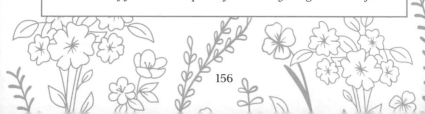

PHYSICAL HEALING:
TAKING CARE OF YOUR TEMPLE

While Jesus walked the face of this earth, He healed many people. The Bible clearly shows that healing is an important gift from God: "Is anyone among you sick? Let him call for the elders of the church, and let them pray over him, anointing him with oil in the name of the Lord. And the prayer of faith will save the sick, and the Lord will raise him up. And if he has committed sins, he will be forgiven" (James 5:14–15 NKJV). "Therefore strengthen the hands which hang down, and the feeble knees, and make straight paths for your feet, so that what is lame may not be dislocated, but rather be healed" (Hebrews 12:12–13 NKJV).

God has given each person a unique physical body. First Corinthians 6:19 reminds us that our body is the temple of the Holy Spirit. His Word instructs us to take care of our temple (body). When we become a Christian, our body belongs to the Lord, and we need to honor Him by taking care of what He has given us.

We can care for our bodies in several ways—proper rest, adequate exercise, and good nutrition. If we neglect our temple, we can't function as we should. To worship, serve others, and follow God's leading, it's important to take care of our physical, emotional, and spiritual needs.

"For you were bought at a price; therefore glorify God in your body and in your spirit, which are God's" (1 Corinthians 6:20 NKJV).

FROM A DISTANCE

A woman in the crowd had suffered for twelve years with constant bleeding, and she could find no cure. Coming up behind Jesus, she touched the fringe of his robe. Immediately, the bleeding stopped.

LUKE 8:43–44 NLT

Perhaps you feel alone in your heartache and brokenness. You wonder if anyone even sees or cares about what you're going through.

No doubt the woman with the issue of blood felt the same. For years she had struggled with health complications. Years of bleeding. Years of humiliation, ostracized from society. Years of feeling different, wishing for a different life, a different situation.

No doubt her emotional health was as poor as her physical health.

And then. . .Jesus. She saw Him from a distance and knew she had to make a move in His direction. Through the crowd she went, pushing, nudging, working her way toward the healer. And when she reached out to touch the hem of His garment, Jesus realized at once and said, "Who touched Me?" The scripture says that He felt virtue going out of Him.

Maybe you feel like that woman. You're viewing Jesus from a distance. Through the crowd. Today, run to Him. Run with the assurance that He loves you and will pour Himself out on your behalf.

I know what it's like to press through the crowd to touch You, Jesus! I'm so grateful You welcome me every time. Amen.

PRAYER JAR INSPIRATION:

God is my healer.

158

TENACIOUS FRIENDS

So they carried him up on the roof, made an opening in the
tiles, and let him down on his bed into the middle of the group
in front of Jesus. When Jesus saw how much faith they had,
he said to the man, "Your sins are forgiven, my friend."

LUKE 5:19–20 GNT

The man lay on a crudely made stretcher, his body racked with pain. He pinched his eyes shut as his friends lifted the stretcher up, up, up to the top of the building. Inside, he could hear voices. Jesus, the one they called Messiah, was speaking.

Right now, though? His thoughts were only on one thing: this crazy scheme cooked up by his well-meaning friends. As they stretched him out on the rooftop, they went to work, creating a hole. Then, as he held his breath, they lowered his stretcher down, down, down to the center of the room, where Jesus looked his way and smiled.

And in that smile the man saw it all: hope, joy, mercy, healing. All his fears and traumas washed away as the Savior took steps in his direction and extended His hand. And, as healing flowed through his body, joy took hold. All his yesterdays now washed away, the man rose and gave himself over to the celebration.

Can you sense it? Can you feel it? What joy must have transpired in the room that day! And what joy when Jesus heals you too!

Thank You for the kind of friends who refuse to give up, Jesus!

PRAYER JAR INSPIRATION:

Who are my most tenacious friends?

FACE TO THE WALL

And it happened, before Isaiah had gone out into the middle court, that the word of the LORD came to him, saying, "Return and tell Hezekiah the leader of My people, 'Thus says the LORD, the God of David your father: "I have heard your prayer, I have seen your tears; surely I will heal you. On the third day you shall go up to the house of the LORD." ' "

2 KINGS 20:4–5 NKJV

Hezekiah lay on his deathbed, face to the wall. No doubt his spirits were low as he asked, "Is this really how things are going to end for me? After years of faithfulness?" While others in Judah had turned their back on God and embraced pagan lifestyles, this man had not. And now here he was, mortally ill.

Side note: It's never good when people refer to you as mortally ill. It sounds so hopeless.

Hezekiah turned his face to the wall and prayed, reminding God of how he had lived a holy life. And God sent Isaiah the prophet to tell Hezekiah to dry his tears because God was going to extend his life by fifteen years.

Wow! An additional fifteen years!

No matter what you're going through, God knows the number of your days. He sees where you're at. And He has a plan for your human body. So go right ahead. Pour out your heart to Him. He's listening. And He's going to guide you every step of the way.

I will trust You, even with my face to the wall, Jesus. Amen.

PRAYER JAR INSPIRATION:

*Even when my face is to the wall,
God still sees and hears my every cry.*

A GOOD NIGHT'S SLEEP

*I lie down and sleep; I wake again, because the L*ORD *sustains me.*

PSALM 3:5 NIV

Sleep is a wonderful thing. But if you're like many twenty-first-century people, you don't get enough. Then you wonder why you're not healing (physically or psychologically) like you should. You're not playing fair with your body!

God designed our bodies to heal while we're sleeping. How can that happen when you're staying up too late or falling asleep with a TV show blasting in the background?

Physical rest is critical, not just to your body, but your mind as well. Muddy, foggy thoughts come on the tail end of a poor night's sleep.

So strategize! Plan for a better night's sleep. Take a warm bubble bath, put on your coziest jammies, take that melatonin, and climb between clean sheets in your warm bed and turn out the light.

And the TV. And the laptop. And your phone. And every other electronic device or distraction. Your body will thank you in the morning!

I confess, I don't always prioritize sleep, Lord. Thank
You for reminding me how important it is! Amen.

PRAYER JAR INSPIRATION:

Sleep is one of the best gifts I can give myself.

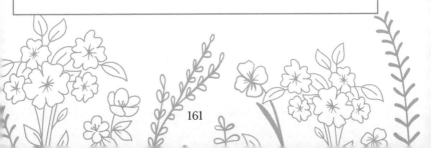

PATIENT ENDURANCE

*"I know your works, your love and faith and service and patient
endurance, and that your latter works exceed the first."*
REVELATION 2:19 ESV

One of the problems with rushed living is that you don't have time to slow down long enough to make sure you're taking care of yourself. Oh, you've done the laundry for the kids. You've driven them to ball practice. Made sure your husband had what he needed for that big meeting at work. Paid the bills. Talked to your daughter's teacher. Fed the puppy. Cleaned up after the puppy.

But you're wiped out. And no one seems to notice. You barely have time to notice yourself. So you grab a quick snack to take the edge off the hunger from skipping lunch, and you put up with the ache in your belly.

Too many years of living like this will take a serious toll on your health, so maybe it's time to slow down long enough to analyze—really analyze—where you stand health-wise. It might be time for some significant changes so that you can live a long, healthy life. (And let's face it—what's the point in taking care of others if you risk your own health?)

*I get it, Jesus. I'll pay more attention to my own health needs
so I'm here for my loved ones even longer. Amen.*

PRAYER JAR INSPIRATION:

My exhaustion is a sign that I need to take better care of myself.

TAKE CARE OF YOU

*Surely you know that you are God's
temple and that God's Spirit lives in you!*

1 CORINTHIANS 3:16 GNT

Imagine you've offered to cook fried chicken for a church event or other gathering. You purchase the chicken. You dip it in milk and eggs then dredge it in flour and seasonings. Afterward you drop it into the pan filled with hot oil, and it begins to sizzle.

But things go catastrophically wrong at that point. Turns out you have the oil too hot. The chicken is cooked on the outside, but when you cut into a piece, it's raw and bloody on the inside.

Sometimes that's how we get after going through traumas. We look overbaked on the outside (the pain of what we've been through shows), but we're raw and oozing on the inside. We hope no one notices what's hiding down deep under the surface.

It's time to take a rest, to make sure you deal with the interior. Your body is a holy thing, created by God, and meant to be treated fairly. Give it the attention it deserves.

*When things have been too hot in my life, I will take
time to cool down with Your help, Jesus.*

PRAYER JAR INSPIRATION:

*My body is the temple of the Holy Spirit,
and it's time I started living like it!*

SCABS SERVE A PURPOSE

*News about him spread all over Syria, and people brought
to him all who were ill with various diseases, those
suffering severe pain, the demon-possessed, those having
seizures, and the paralyzed; and he healed them.*

MATTHEW 4:24 NIV

Stop picking at it!

Remember as a kid when you would scrape up your knee? Mom would put some medicine on it (maybe antibiotic cream) and then slap a bandage on it. "Now, don't mess with it!" she would say.

And you tried. You really, really tried. But the temptation was too strong, especially after the bandage fell off and you saw that scab. So you picked at it. And guess what? It started bleeding all over again.

That's how it is with emotional and psychological wounds too. When you allow the salve of the Holy Spirit to do its work, healing comes over time. But if you pull off God's protective layering and begin to pick at it, reliving it over and over again, it will never heal.

Leave that bandage on. Give God time. Resist the temptation to fix this yourself. Scabs serve a purpose. Leave them alone.

*You are trying to heal me, Lord, and sometimes I
make it worse instead of better. Give me the courage
to leave this situation in Your hands. Amen.*

PRAYER JAR INSPIRATION:

I will leave my healing in God's capable hands.

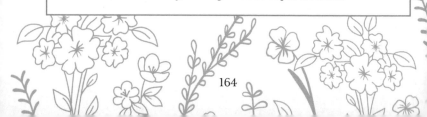

A TEMPLE OF HIS SPIRIT

*Do you not know that your bodies are temples of the Holy Spirit, who
is in you, whom you have received from God? You are not your own;
you were bought at a price. Therefore honor God with your bodies.*

1 CORINTHIANS 6:19–20 NIV

As wars heat up across the planet, we see more of an emphasis on
houses of worship being targeted. When temples are destroyed, it hits
the heart of the people.

The enemy has always been one to go after the thing that matters,
and that's particularly true when he comes after your temple (your
physical body). There's usually no fair warning when the attacks come.
Bombs go off, and you're incapacitated, staggering around, wondering
when the walls will rise again.

This is particularly true if you've been battling a lengthy illness
or you're in the fight of your life to regain your health after a cancer
diagnosis. The enemy works overtime to hit the temple because he
sees it as the most valuable (and therefore, the most important) place
to take down. If he can destroy your health and convince you that you
won't recover, you'll lie among the rubble, defeated.

God wants you to rise up. Even if you can't do it physically, rise
up in your spirit and say to the enemy, "No! You have no authority
here! This temple belongs to the Most High God!"

My temple belongs to You, Lord! Amen.

PRAYER JAR INSPIRATION:

My temple houses the Spirit of God!

PUPPY LOVE

The righteous care for the needs of their animals,
but the kindest acts of the wicked are cruel.

PROVERBS 12:10 NIV

If you're struggling with anxiety or stress, try spending time with the animal kingdom. No, really. A lapdog or playful kitten can be a wonderful stress reliever.

Stroking that pup's fur, getting sweet puppy kisses—these things are simple at face value. But they can go a long way in making you feel better on a day when everything seems to be falling apart.

If you don't have a pet of your own, then turn on a video of puppies playing or kittens chasing one another. You'll feel better in no time.

God created the animal kingdom for us. And today's verse is a reminder that we have an obligation to these darling creatures that minister to us so beautifully. We are to love them, tend to them, and care for their needs. This is such a small thing to ask for all they give to us.

It's a love-love relationship!

Thank You for giving us puppies, kittens, and all of the
other wonderful animals in Your kingdom, Lord. They
are such a blessing and soften our hearts. Amen.

PRAYER JAR INSPIRATION:

Pets are a blessing—a gift from God!

YOU CAN HAVE PEACE

"Peace I leave with you; my peace I give you. I do not give to you as the world gives. Do not let your hearts be troubled and do not be afraid."

JOHN 14:27 NIV

Imagine you were tasked with baking an angel food cake for a family get-together. You gathered your ingredients and whipped it up, but something went terribly wrong and the cake fell flat. After a bit of research, you realized you left out a key ingredient—egg whites.

Egg whites are a critical part of making an angel food cake. (This cake relies on the whipped whites because it has no baking powder in it.)

That example might seem a little silly, but an angel food cake without its egg whites is a bit like you when you're stressed. Without peace (picture those fluffy egg whites) you simply can't function. Everything falls flat.

Today God can give you peace, even if you have been missing it in your life for a very long time. He can bring healing to your soul and can wash over you with the peace of His Spirit. When He does, everything will come back into alignment. (In other words, the cake will bake beautifully!)

*No matter what I'm going through, I can
have peace, Lord—with Your help! Amen.*

PRAYER JAR INSPIRATION:

God gives peace as a gift.

WATCHMEN ON THE WALL

*"For where two or three are gathered in
my name, there am I among them."*

MATTHEW 18:20 ESV

In biblical times, cities were fortified with high walls so that enemies couldn't come in and take them by force.

If you picture your body, your vessel, as a city, you can see some similarities. Sometimes the enemy (sickness, disease) tries to rush the walls and take over. When that happens, it can leave the city (you!) in disarray.

That's why it's so important to have watchmen on the wall. Having a team of prayer warriors can be a critical part of your journey as you work your way toward physical healing. They will do the hard work of fighting back the enemy while you take the time to heal.

There's power in numbers. And when you have a team of believers working together, praying together, believing together—watch out! Miracles can happen when you have a solid group of watchmen on the wall.

When I'm in need, I will gather my team of watchmen, Lord! Amen.

PRAYER JAR INSPIRATION:

Who are my watchmen on the wall?

LIFE TO YOUR
MORTAL BODY

*And if the Spirit of him who raised Jesus from the dead is living
in you, he who raised Christ from the dead will also give life to
your mortal bodies because of his Spirit who lives in you.*

ROMANS 8:11 NIV

Checking your weight. Checking your blood sugar. Checking your blood pressure. Having annual physicals. Getting routine labs done. Why do you suppose these are so important?

For the same reason it's critical to take your car in for oil changes! If you overlook something as simple as an oil change, the engine can burn up. And if you deliberately overlook small health matters, they can escalate into large ones.

It's not a good thing to ignore the little problems, thinking they won't catch up to you. They will. And it's not good to live blinded to these things either. So, if you've been putting off a doctor's visit, let this be a sign to make an appointment. Stop waiting. Stop wondering. Do the practical things and invite God into them. He will be right there to help you now, while the problems (if any) are small.

*I will take better care of myself, Lord, and
bring life to my mortal body. Amen.*

PRAYER JAR INSPIRATION:

*Little problems can become big problems
if I don't nip them in the bud.*

HIS COMMANDMENTS
ARE NOT BURDENSOME

For this is the love of God, that we keep his commandments.
And his commandments are not burdensome.

1 JOHN 5:3 ESV

When you're low on vitamin D, the doctor tells you to spend more time in the sunshine. When you're low on iron, he (or she) encourages you to eat more iron-rich foods like liver, beef, or eggs. Good foods can bring healing.

A lot of our medical woes in the twenty-first century come from wear and tear. Too much time on the computer causes eye strain, which leads to headaches and neck pain. Too many hours lounging on the sofa streaming movies leads to laziness or unwillingness to take that daily walk with your friend. French fries and chocolate pie taste great but raise your blood sugar.

You get the idea. But the answers to most of these things come in the form of one simple word: *Obedience.*

Obedience gets up off the sofa.

Obedience pushes the chair away from the table.

Obedience steps out into the sunshine and breathes the fresh air.

Obedience leads to health.

Disobedience? Well, you probably already know where it leads.

Your commandments are for my well-being, Lord! Amen.

PRAYER JAR INSPIRATION:

God's commandments are never a burden.

I'LL MAKE UP FOR IT

*"But seek first his kingdom and his righteousness,
and all these things will be given to you as well."*

MATTHEW 6:33 NIV

When we're in a crazy-busy season, we sometimes say things like, "I'll make up for it on the weekend. I'll sleep in on Saturday."

Then Friday night comes and we're up till the wee hours watching a movie or TV show. We eventually fall sleep and wake up feeling awful—stiff and sore from too many hours in bed. And we feel a little hungover.

The problem with living like this for too long is that it can affect our physical and mental well-being. It's hard to be nice to others when we're achy, tired, and cranky most of the time. And let's face it—we never really make up for the crazy-busy workweek. Saturdays are often packed full of house cleaning, laundry, and so on. And Sundays? If you're part of a church (especially if you have little ones), Sunday can be the most stressful day of the week.

It's better to keep a balance as the week goes on, to avoid the highs and lows of sleep deprivation. So do your best to spread things out so you're not faced with an avalanche in the end!

*I will do my best to keep my life in balance, Lord,
but I'm going to need Your help. Amen.*

PRAYER JAR INSPIRATION:

Balance is key, and God will help me find it.

YOUR PROVISION

And my God will supply every need of yours according
to his riches in glory in Christ Jesus.

PHILIPPIANS 4:19 ESV

There's an interesting story in the Old Testament of a widow and her son. The prophet Elijah visited her during a lean season in her life. What did he ask for? Basically, a meal. He wanted water and a piece of bread.

The woman had just enough oil and flour to bake a loaf of bread for herself and her son. But she didn't hesitate. She was prepared to use the last of her ingredients to do as the prophet asked. But then something miraculous happened! God supernaturally supplied more oil and flour. The empty jar was suddenly full. And the jar of oil never ran out either.

This is what happens when you place your trust in God, not man. That friend you've been leaning on? She can only take you so far. That job you put all your stock in? It's not your provider. God is your source, and He will provide in ways no one else possibly can. So turn your eyes upon Jesus. He's the one who will see you through.

You are my provider, Lord! I will keep
my eyes on You, not others. Amen.

PRAYER JAR INSPIRATION:

God will supply all my needs.

172

MY BODY, MY TEMPLE

Or do you not know that your body is a temple of the Holy Spirit within you, whom you have from God? You are not your own, for you were bought with a price. So glorify God in your body.

1 Corinthians 6:19–20 esv

Why do you suppose God called the human body a temple? What does that mean, exactly? A temple is a holy place, a set-apart place. No one would dare desecrate a temple. If an enemy came through the village, perhaps the worst insult of all would be destruction of the temple.

With those things in mind, it's getting easier to see why God called our bodies a temple. Each of us only has one, and we are to treat it with the reverence and respect we would treat the sanctuary of our church.

We wouldn't fill the sanctuary with trash or forget to vacuum the floors. We would make sure every light bulb was in place, the sound system was in working order, and the chairs or pews were in great shape to hold the incoming congregation.

These might seem like little details, but they're like taking care of your physical body. Exercise, vitamins, healthy foods, quiet time, adequate sleep—these are all things to keep your temple running smoothly!

Help me remember to care for this temple, Jesus. You've only given me one body, and I want to take excellent care of it. Amen.

PRAYER JAR INSPIRATION:

My temple is a holy place.

SELF-ESTEEM?

For it is not the one who commends himself who is approved, but the one whom the Lord commends.

2 CORINTHIANS 10:18 ESV

Pop psychologists and influencers talk a lot about self-esteem. According to their sage advice, self-esteem is critical. You have to have it to thrive in this world. And so a lot of people look to themselves to heal. They follow the advice of the pros but don't find healing. Why?

The truth is, we can't heal ourselves. The answers were never inside of us, no matter how terrific we think we are. We must fix our eyes not on ourselves but on Jesus. We need God-esteem if we're ever going to recover.

And when we realize God's deep love for us and His passion to see us healed and whole, we do become more confident from the inside-out. Not because of anything we've done but because of what He did for us when He gave His life on the cross.

It's not a bad thing to love yourself. You were created in the image of God, after all. But to look at yourself as being all-knowing? That's just not wise.

I look to You, Jesus! I will have God-esteem! Amen.

PRAYER JAR INSPIRATION:

I can't find the answers inside myself.
I must look to the heavenly Father.

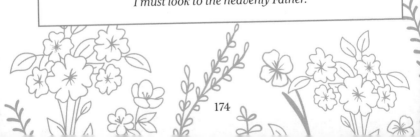

SPIRITUAL
HEALING

When we're broken physically, we go to the doctor. When we're broken spiritually, we should turn to God for help. He's in the healing business and wants to mend what is broken.

Jeremiah 18:4 (NKJV) says, "And the vessel that he made of clay was marred in the hand of the potter; so he made it again into another vessel, as it seemed good to the potter to make."

God has the power to break and remake our lives into that which will give Him glory. So how do we mend what's broken?

1. Through a healthy diet of God's Word. Scripture is powerful. It penetrates our heart and shows us the way to live our lives. His Word is good medicine and beneficial for spiritual healing.

2. By being still. Sometimes we get busy and don't stay still long enough to hear God's voice or allow Him to heal our hearts. The first part of Psalm 46:10 (NKJV) says, "Be still, and know that I am God." I have that verse displayed in my office. I appreciate the reminder to be still so I can hear His voice.

3. Allow the blood of Jesus to heal what's broken. Without the blood Jesus shed when He died on the cross, there would be no forgiveness for our sins: "Who Himself bore our sins in His own body on the tree, that we, having died to sin, might live for righteousness—by whose stripes you were healed" (1 Peter 2:24 NKJV).

WE ALL FALL SHORT

For all have sinned and fall short of the glory of God.

ROMANS 3:23 NIV

So many believers come to faith in Jesus after living hard lives. They bring with them years of baggage and (oftentimes) guilt over the pain they've caused others and themselves.

This guilt can be debilitating if you don't let go of it. Jesus died for all of it, even the stuff you're incredibly ashamed of. So let your heart be mended. Let the guilt absolve. Do what you need to do to make things right with the people you've hurt, but don't allow the shame of yesterday to keep you from living in faith and hope today.

Take another look at today's verse: We all sin. We all fall short. You didn't win some sort of award for being the worst-possible human before you gave your heart to Jesus. Everyone was just as messed up as you.

But God. . .

Those two words change everything—about your situation and your heart. God is the great healer of all broken things, and He sent His Son so that you could experience full spiritual healing.

So let it go. Yesterday is gone. Today is brand-new!

*I've been ashamed of my past, Jesus, but You
died to save me from my yesterdays! Amen.*

PRAYER JAR INSPIRATION:

The blood of Jesus covers every sin, no matter how grievous.

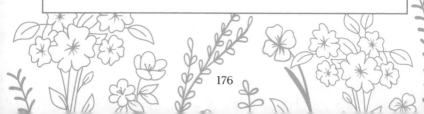

WEEDS IN THE GARDEN

Jesus told them another parable: "The kingdom of heaven is like a man who sowed good seed in his field. But while everyone was sleeping, his enemy came and sowed weeds among the wheat, and went away. When the wheat sprouted and formed heads, then the weeds also appeared."

MATTHEW 13:24–26 NIV

Your spiritual life is like a garden filled with lovely flowers planted by the Lord. He has a lot in store for you, and it all starts with spiritual growth. The water of His Spirit. The fertilizer of His Word. Apply these things, and you'll do fine.

The problem is that gardens are often overrun with pesky things that don't belong there: weeds, pests, fungi. All these icky things can take over, ruining a perfectly good crop.

The same is true when you allow the enemy to enter your spiritual garden. He threatens to drown out the good with the bad. Before you realize it, poor theology has grown up: "God doesn't love me. God isn't fair. God must be mad at me." You name it, the enemy will try to get you to believe it.

Only these are lies. God does love you. God is just. God isn't the tiniest bit angry at you.

These little beliefs, false as they are, become weeds in your spiritual garden, and they must go. Otherwise, healing will never come. (How could you convince a child to heal of a rift with a parent if they truly believed the parent couldn't stand them?)

Weed the garden. Get rid of the stuff crowding out the truth.

I will do my best to keep the garden free of weeds, Lord. Amen.

PRAYER JAR INSPIRATION:

It's weeding day!

CONTEND FOR THE FAITH

Dear friends, although I was very eager to write to you about the salvation we share, I felt compelled to write and urge you to contend for the faith that was once for all entrusted to God's holy people.

JUDE 1:3 NIV

The world is full of people who have given up on God. Perhaps they have grown weary of waiting for an answer to prayer. Or maybe they're angry over the way they were treated at a church and have turned their anger to the Lord.

There are all sorts of reasons why previously strong Christians turn their backs on God, but here's the good news: He never turns His back on us, even when we're angry at Him or have completely given up on our faith.

There's a reason the English poet Francis Thompson called God "the hound of heaven." He keeps pursuing, keeps loving, keeps chasing you down even when you're hiding away, hoping not to be caught.

Keep praying for those who've given up on the Lord. And if you're struggling in this area yourself, be reminded today that He still loves you, still wants you, still plans to move in your life. Open yourself back up to the possibilities if you can. Contend for your faith. Fight for it.

My faith is worth fighting for, Lord! You've entrusted it to me, and I will battle for it. Amen.

PRAYER JAR INSPIRATION:

The fight for faith is one battle worth fighting.

HEALED PEOPLE
HEAL PEOPLE

*Lord, I have heard of your fame; I stand in awe of
your deeds, Lord. Repeat them in our day, in our time
make them known; in wrath remember mercy.*

HABAKKUK 3:2 NIV

It's no surprise that so many people who've been through the wringer
end up going into counseling. Once you've survived a trauma and thrived
on the other end of it, you have a story to tell. You also have lessons
learned that could be beneficial to others. Healed people heal people.

Think about it this way: when you're going through an unexpected
and unwanted divorce, who do you turn to for counsel? Probably
someone who's walked that road ahead of you. Why? Because she
(somehow) made it through, and you know she's going to share from
her journey.

More than anything, she's going to give you hope that you'll be
fine on the opposite side of this. And, admit it, hope is a precious
commodity when you're in the trenches. You don't need Debby Downer
sharing her woe-is-me stories. You need Patty Pep-Me-Up giving you
words of encouragement and life.

One day that will be you. You'll be the one sharing and caring.
Until then, hold tight to those who've already walked the road.

*One day that will be me, Jesus. I'll be the one sharing my story.
Heal me so that I can encourage others to heal, I pray. Amen.*

PRAYER JAR INSPIRATION:

I will make it through this.

179

WE ALL NEED THE SAVIOR

*Because, if you confess with your mouth that Jesus is Lord and believe
in your heart that God raised him from the dead, you will be saved.*

ROMANS 10:9 ESV

Spiritual healing comes when you recognize your need for a Savior and place your life (and heart) into His capable hands. No matter where you've been, no matter what you've done, no matter how heinous your sins, that simple act of conforming to His image changes everything.

But it's a process to accept forgiveness. You'll probably still beat yourself up for the things you did wrong in the past. You might still have regrets. There might even be some things you still have to make right (people you need to apologize to).

But understanding that God now sees you, not as a sinner, but as a precious child purchased by the blood of His Son? Well, that's something to celebrate! And that news is so good that it's worth sharing with others so that they can come to know this amazing Savior too.

*Accepting You was the best decision of my life, Jesus. Allowing You
to break away the cobwebs surrounding my heart, letting You heal
the broken places, accepting Your forgiveness—these decisions
have changed me for all eternity, and I'm so grateful. Amen.*

PRAYER JAR INSPIRATION:

I can proclaim salvation's message of hope!

LEARNING TO TRUST

Those who know your name trust in you, for you,
Lord, have never forsaken those who seek you.

PSALM 9:10 NIV

Part of the spiritual healing journey is simply learning to trust God again. If you've been disappointed and have pointed the finger at Him (say, after the death of a loved one or a tragic financial loss), it's easier just to go on distrusting. To place your hand in His again is tough.

But it's important. Because God isn't the one who let you down. We live in a fallen world where bad things happen to good people. And God still cares very deeply when you're hurting, so the last thing you need to do is pull away from Him.

Draw close. Even if it's hard. *Especially* if it's hard. He's right there, hand extended, ready to relight the flame that once burned bright between you.

It's going to be a process, Lord, but I want to learn to trust You again.
I'll confess, there have been moments when my faith wavered, when
my trust gave way to fear. But You have never abandoned me, and
I know You never will. So I choose to trust You today. Amen.

PRAYER JAR INSPIRATION:

I can learn to trust again.

A SERVANT'S HEART

As each has received a gift, use it to serve one another,
as good stewards of God's varied grace.

1 PETER 4:10 ESV

"I don't want anything to do with your God."

Maybe you've heard those words from a family member, friend, or neighbor. They see you coming, all bright-eyed and bushy-tailed, and put up a hand of warning: "Don't come over here spouting off your religious messages. I'm not interested."

That hard-heartedness has led many to lives of misery and isolation. But there are ways beyond those high fences they're building.

Take a pot of chicken soup when your friend is sick.

Let your neighbor know you're praying when her spouse leaves.

Offer to mow that elderly neighbor's lawn when she gripes that no one sees her or cares about her anymore.

Acts of service are an amazing way to show God's love. (And let's face it: there's almost always something you can do to share His love with a lost and dying world if you're really paying attention.)

So, buy groceries for that single mom. Go ahead. And send a kind handwritten note to that grumpy man down the street, along with a plate of cookies. Watch those walls fall as you extend a hand of love to this hurting world.

Give me a servant's heart, Lord. Amen.

PRAYER JAR INSPIRATION:

When I don't know what else to do, I can always serve others.

LEGALISM

Yet we know that a person is put right with God only through faith in Jesus Christ, never by doing what the Law requires. We, too, have believed in Christ Jesus in order to be put right with God through our faith in Christ, and not by doing what the Law requires. For no one is put right with God by doing what the Law requires.

GALATIANS 2:16 GNT

Were you raised in church? If so, what "brand" (or flavor) was it? Some churches are thriving bodies, perfect for raising kids. Others are slightly off-balance, pushing works above grace (or even the other way around, condoning all sorts of sinful lifestyle choices while claiming the Bible isn't relevant for today).

Where we've come from can affect where we are. And let's face it—churches are sometimes a hotbed for strife and confusion if they veer off from the intent of the Word of God.

If you were raised in a church that contributed to your brokenness instead of seeking to fix it, there's still time to turn things around. You can make sure your children are raised in a healing place. It's possible to bring them up in an environment where the Bible has top priority, but grace is displayed in all situations as well.

Balance, as always, is key.

I love Your Word, Lord. And I want my behavior to reflect that. But I don't want to be bound by legalism. Show me how to live by faith and display Your love to this hungry world. Amen.

PRAYER JAR INSPIRATION:

Authentic faith leads to good works.

DON'T BUY THE WORLD'S BRAND OF SPIRITUAL HEALING

Dear friends, do not believe every spirit, but test the spirits to see whether they are from God, because many false prophets have gone out into the world.

1 JOHN 4:1 NIV

If you look up the words *spiritual healing* online, you'll find all sorts of crazy suggestions. The majority of these come from new age sources that don't believe in the Bible. And their remedies for healing are as odd as their sources. They include things like crystals, vibrations, and atmospheric energy, as well as New Age meditation and visualization. Strange and scary stuff.

We know that we live in a fallen world and that the enemy will do everything he can to offer counterfeits. These fall into that category. The problem with all those things is that they don't offer real solutions.

Genuine spiritual brokenness requires healing from the one who created you. God pieced you together in your mother's womb. In fact, the Bible says He knew you even before the foundation of the world. Wouldn't it make more sense to trust your spirit to Him instead of some random crystals on the countertop? Best of all, God adores you. He has your best interest at heart. So turn away from worldly things and place your heart in His hands.

Thank You for giving me discernment, Lord! Amen.

PRAYER JAR INSPIRATION:

Only the real deal for me—that's Jesus!

SHACKLES

*Truly I am your servant, LORD; I serve you just as my
mother did; you have freed me from my chains.*

PSALM 116:16 NIV

In biblical times, prisoners were bound with shackles around their ankles and wrists. The shackles ensured the prisoner wouldn't get very far if he tried to run.

The enemy of your soul has his own brand of shackles. He grips you with guilt and condemnation. Just about the time you think you've been set free (and you have), he convinces you that you're still shackled to those terrible feelings of shame and guilt.

But you're not! When Jesus died on the cross, He broke every chain. Every single one. Nothing holds you bound anymore. It's just an illusion. And let's face it: Satan is the master of illusions. He's great at bluffing!

There are no shackles on you. None. You can walk freely! The guilt from yesterday's sins is long gone now. You can walk in total freedom, shackle-free!

*It feels so good to be relieved of the guilt and shame, Lord!
I could never have freed myself. But Your sacrifice on the
cross accomplished it all! How grateful I am. Amen.*

PRAYER JAR INSPIRATION:

My chains are broken!

SUNLIGHT

*But if we walk in the light, as he is in the light,
we have fellowship with one another, and the
blood of Jesus his Son cleanses us from all sin.*

1 John 1:7 esv

If you've lived in a dank, dark prison cell for any length of time, the sunlight can be blinding. You squint and put your hand over your eyes to protect them from the glare. And for a moment—just a moment—you contemplate running back into that cell to avoid the pain of adjusting.

But you don't. You forge ahead, allowing your eyes time to adjust.

The same is true when your spirit is first coming alive to the truth of the gospel message. Some of it might seem a little too glaring. You squint and squirm, wondering if you've made the right decision. Following Jesus might be tougher than you thought.

Oh, but it's worth it. Once your eyes are fully opened to the truth, shackles fall. You see clearly, and it all makes sense. And before long the light becomes your friend, not a hindrance. In fact, you're so open to it that you can't wait to share it with others who are enduring their own prison cells.

Walk free in the light, friend!

You are the light, Jesus. So, if I stick close to You, I will always walk in the light. Thank You for the freedom that Your light brings. Amen.

PRAYER JAR INSPIRATION:

My spiritual eyes can (and will) adjust to the truth of God's Word.

BY HIS WOUNDS YOU HAVE BEEN HEALED

"He himself bore our sins" in his body on the cross,
so that we might die to sins and live for righteousness;
"by his wounds you have been healed."

1 PETER 2:24 NIV

Jesus was never content just to bring physical healing. He usually followed up with a spiritual message. For what would be the point of having blind eyes opened if not to also open spiritual eyes? And what would be the point of lame legs walking if not to walk in the newness of life?

What would be the point of eyes opened if not opened to truth? And what would be the point of a mute tongue speaking if not to speak words of life?

Jesus cares about every aspect of your life, inside and out. He wants to see you healed in every single area, not one stone unturned. Why? So that you can live your fullest, healthiest life, complete and whole.

Today's verse shares a remarkable truth: it was Jesus' wounds that brought healing for our bodies, souls, and spirits. Because He went to the cross, because He bore the pain of the beatings and nails in His hands and feet, we have healing today. What a remarkable sacrifice on the part of our Savior!

I'll never be able to thank You for what You did for me, Jesus,
but I'm so grateful for the wounds that brought my healing. Amen.

PRAYER JAR INSPIRATION:

By His wounds I am healed.

187

A BINDER OF WOUNDS

He heals the brokenhearted and binds up their wounds.

PSALM 147:3 NIV

If you sustained injuries on the battleground but had no one to bind them, what would happen? You would bleed out, for sure. The medic, who appears from out of nowhere to bind your wounds, is ultimately the one who saves your life.

Jesus is the binder of wounds. Whenever you sustain an injury of any kind—emotional, mental, or spiritual, He's right there, ready to jump in and save you. You don't have to hope He shows up; He *always* shows up. And you don't have to give Him instructions. He knows just what to do.

He's the ultimate medic with supernatural vision and unlimited healing capabilities. You can trust Him with your body. You can trust Him with your thoughts. You can trust Him with your heart.

You can trust Him. Period. He's always there at just the right moment and knows just what to do.

You're the ultimate wound-binder, Lord! My chances of survival went way up the moment I placed my life in Your hands. Amen.

PRAYER JAR INSPIRATION:

My medic, Jesus, is on the way!

A JOYFUL HEART

A cheerful heart is good medicine, but a broken
spirit saps a person's strength.
PROVERBS 17:22 NLT

When you've been sick with an infection for more than a couple of days, visiting the doctor is inevitable. And once she writes that prescription, you can almost feel yourself getting better, even before you've swallowed that first tablet. The promise of medication gives you hope, even before it takes effect.

The Bible has a prescription that works wonders on a broken heart or troubled spirit: joy. When you apply joy—as you would swallow that antibiotic—you feel better. Much better. And here's the good news: joy works even faster than medication, which must get into your system before it begins to have an effect. Joy offers an instantaneous lift!

No matter what you're struggling with today, pray for joy. When it floods over you, you're going to feel much, much better.

I love the joy-filled people You've placed in my life,
Lord. I want to be more like that. Fill me to overflowing
so that I can spill over onto those I love. Amen.

PRAYER JAR INSPIRATION:

My goal is to radiate the joy of Jesus around my friends.

LOVE, THE GREAT HEALER

And now these three remain: faith, hope and
love. But the greatest of these is love.
1 CORINTHIANS 13:13 NIV

Why do you suppose the Bible teaches us that love is the "greatest thing"? It's greater than faith. It's greater than hope. And both of those things are amazing all by themselves!

But love is greater. It has the power to transform hearts, lives, and situations.

Love can heal relationships. Love can heal a broken heart. Love can heal a wounded spirit. Love can heal. . .pretty much anything.

Jesus shared the greatest example of love when He gave His life for us on Calvary. In that one act, He performed an act of love that surpasses all others. And as He did, He asked something of us: "Will you show (and share) My love with others?"

It's not a big task when you think about it. Sharing the good news is sharing a story of hope and healing. You really can change the lives of those around you simply by sharing the story of what Jesus did for them two thousand years ago on the cross at Calvary.

I am a good-news-bearer when I share Your story with people
around me, Lord! Thank You for Your sacrifice on the cross,
not just for my sins but for the sins of all mankind. Amen.

PRAYER JAR INSPIRATION:

Through my story of hope and healing,
I can bring hope and healing to others.

DON'T BE TROUBLED

"Do not let your hearts be troubled.
You believe in God; believe also in me."

JOHN 14:1 NIV

Whenever the disciples were stressed out, Jesus brought them back to center with this phrase: "Don't let your hearts be troubled. You believe in God; believe also in me." They had the God of the universe physically traveling side by side with them! Can you imagine? And yet they still got stressed out at times.

Think about this: before Jesus came, the Jews had a long-standing relationship with God, but they couldn't see Him with their eyes or hear Him with their ears. They trusted in the law and in all they had learned from their religious rituals.

But law and rituals will only take you so far. When you're hurting, when you're stressed, it helps to have the living, breathing God of the universe standing directly in front of you.

You might not see Jesus with your own eyes like the disciples did, but He's right there, hand tightly clasping yours. As with those great men of old, He's walking and talking with you.

So take a deep breath. It might feel like you're going through this alone, but you are not.

You walk with me and talk with me, Lord!
It's remarkable to imagine that the Creator of all
cares about me too! I will put my trust in You! Amen.

PRAYER JAR INSPIRATION:

I can give all my stresses to the heavenly Father.

YOU'RE NOT
THE ONLY ONE

*Even though I walk through the valley of the shadow of death, I will fear
no evil, for you are with me; your rod and your staff, they comfort me.*

PSALM 23:4 ESV

When crises hit, you might feel completely alone. No one you know
has been through the exact same crisis you're going through, and you
wonder if you've been specially chosen for such a terrible journey.

No one else has lost a spouse.

No one else has a child on drugs.

No one else has a son in prison.

It can feel like that; and it might even be true of your friend circle,
but you are certainly not the first to experience this type of tragedy. One
key thing that can help with your healing is to join a support group for
people who are going through the same sort of crisis. GriefShare is a
wonderful program for those who've lost loved ones. DivorceCare is
perfect for someone who has faced an unexpected divorce. Al-Anon
is amazing for family members of addicts.

When you're surrounded by like-minded people, you learn from one
another. And you gain the support of people who know exactly what
you're thinking and feeling because they're thinking and feeling it too.

*Lord, show me who to link arms with so that we can
learn from each other and heal together. Amen.*

PRAYER JAR INSPIRATION:

I'm not the only one facing this problem.

192

KEEP CLIMBING

He will cover you with his pinions, and under his wings you will find
refuge; his faithfulness is a shield and buckler. You will not fear the
terror of the night, nor the arrow that flies by day, nor the pestilence
that stalks in darkness, nor the destruction that wastes at noonday.

PSALM 91:4–6 ESV

Have you ever visited the Statue of Liberty? It's a *l-o-n-g* climb to the top, and there's no other way to get up there. Once you commit to the process, you start climbing. And you keep on climbing until you either (1) reach the top or (2) turn around and head back down.

Recovering from a trauma is a bit like climbing those stairs to the top of the Statue of Liberty. Once you commit, you stay on the stairs until you arrive at the top. And from that lofty place, the view is a lot different than it was down below. From up there, you can see everything. Clearly.

Don't give up on the bottom stairs. Don't give up in the middle when you're out of breath. Stick with it to the very top, where the view will be spectacular. Up there God will give you clarity and insight to bring everything into perspective.

I want to stop sometimes, Lord. But You nudge me
on! Thank You for giving me the tenacity to keep
climbing even when I don't feel like it. Amen.

PRAYER JAR INSPIRATION:

With God's nudging, I can keep going even when I don't feel like it.

INSENSITIVE

Love does no wrong to a neighbor;
therefore love is the fulfilling of the law.
ROMANS 13:10 ESV

Part of the healing journey comes from realizing that not everyone is wired the same. If someone has hurt you with their insensitivity to your problem, don't get worked up for too long. Remember, they might not have the same depth of feeling or emotion for the problem as you do.

Some people simply aren't empaths. They're just not. Even some believers struggle in this area. They're not deliberately trying to hurt you with their insensitivity. They're just oblivious or approaching it from a completely different angle.

One of the joys of understanding the different personality types is that it helps you guard your heart when you bump up against friends who have a radically different take on things.

And here's another great lesson to glean from insensitive people: you can demonstrate the opposite spirit. You can become even more sensitive to the needs of others so that you can better minister to them when they're hurting.

Guard my heart, Jesus. I don't want to overreact when people aren't as sensitive as I hope they'll be. Help me deepen my sensitivity to others so I can show them You love during hard seasons. Amen.

PRAYER JAR INSPIRATION:

I will be more sensitive to the needs of others.

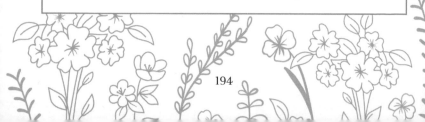

194

YOUR FAITH CAN GROW

*Now faith is confidence in what we hope for and assurance about
what we do not see. This is what the ancients were commended for.*

HEBREWS 11:1–2 NIV

There's a misunderstanding, based in part on errant biblical teaching,
that Christians will be immune to sickness and pain. Some believers
feel that radical faith will keep them from walking through trauma.

Imagine their surprise when traumas come anyway. And when
that faith, no matter how strong, is tested.

God never promised us a pain-free life. We live in a broken, fallen
world, and troubles come in like a flood at times. Our faith is tested.
Our belief system is shaken. But through it all, God remains the same.
If you don't believe it, read Hebrews 11, where you will discover that
great men and women of faith didn't always get what they prayed for.

Your faith will be challenged, but you can come out of life experiences
stronger than ever before. The Lord hasn't promised to keep
you *from* it, but He has promised to walk with you *through* it all.

*When I place my trust in You, I can still have confidence, Jesus,
even when things don't seem to be going my way. Amen.*

PRAYER JAR INSPIRATION:

My faith can grow through life's challenges.

MUSTARD SEED FAITH

"Truly I tell you, if you have faith as small as a mustard seed,
you can say to this mountain, 'Move from here to there,'
and it will move. Nothing will be impossible for you."

MATTHEW 17:20 NIV

We've established that faith is critical to overcoming rough seasons. You might be in the middle of a terrible situation right now and your faith feels small. In fact, you wonder if there's even an ounce of it left after all you've been through.

This would be an excellent time to reread the verse above. The Bible says that faith is like a mustard seed. In case you've never seen one, a mustard seed isn't much bigger than a pen point. It's just a tiny dot of a thing. And yet here Jesus was, telling His disciples that all they needed was a pen point of faith to witness miracles.

Aren't you glad He didn't compare it to a watermelon? Or a cantaloupe, even? It would be easy to come back with, "Well, I sure don't have big faith!"

But He said you don't need big faith. You just need a little. And whether you can see it or not, that tiny sliver of faith still residing in your heart is enough to get you through your rough patch. And best of all, it's going to grow because of what you've been through.

Thank You for helping me through rough seasons,
Jesus. I will place my faith in You. Amen.

PRAYER JAR INSPIRATION:

Mustard seed faith is all I need.

CRISIS OF FAITH

For it is by grace you have been saved, through
faith—and this is not from yourselves, it is the gift
of God—not by works, so that no one can boast.

Ephesians 2:8–9 niv

Even the most faith-filled people sometimes fall into the pit of despair. Jesus' good friends Mary and Martha are prime examples of this. They were personal witnesses to the miraculous things that happened at the hands of the Savior. But when they really needed Him (at the death of their brother, Lazarus), Jesus was busy tending to someone else's needs.

Martha wasn't having it. She gave Jesus a piece of her mind: "If You had been here, this wouldn't have happened."

Sounds a lot like us today! "God, I thought You would show up for me, but You didn't."

Jesus already knew, of course, that He could (and would) raise Lazarus from the dead. And He's pretty good at raising your situations from the depths, as well. Instead of arguing with Martha, He simply went to the tomb and cried out, "Lazarus, come forth!"

If you're in the middle of a faith crisis right now, picture Lazarus coming forth from that tomb, grave clothes falling away. If Jesus would do that for Him, He can certainly resurrect you too!

Lord, I'm thankful that You're still in the business
of peeling away grave clothes! Amen.

PRAYER JAR INSPIRATION:

I can trust Jesus with the resurrection of my faith.

DRAW CLOSE TO HIM

Jesus entered Jericho and was passing through. A man was there
by the name of Zacchaeus; he was a chief tax collector and was
wealthy. He wanted to see who Jesus was, but because he was short
he could not see over the crowd. So he ran ahead and climbed a
sycamore-fig tree to see him, since Jesus was coming that way.

LUKE 19:1–4 NIV

Zacchaeus was a tax collector who lived during Jesus' day. According to this passage from the gospel of Luke, he wasn't a very tall man, so he decided to climb a sycamore tree to watch as Jesus came by.

Nowhere in the story do we get the idea that Zacchaeus was trying to draw attention to himself. In fact, it seems more likely he was up in that tree, hidden away, just to catch a glimpse. (And let's face it: he probably wasn't a favorite with the people in the village, being a tax collector and all.)

But Jesus wasn't content to let Zacchaeus hide away. He stopped, looked right into that tax collector's face, and said, "Come down. I'm going to your house today."

If we were writing this story as an episodic series, we would cut the scene right there and make the audience wait a full week to find out what happened next. A loud gasp must have risen from the crowd as they cried out, "No, Jesus! That's the last place You should go."

But, as was always the case with Jesus, the last place was His first place. And that hasn't changed. No matter who you are or what you've done, He still cries out, "Come on down! I want to hang out with you!"

Jesus, I get it. You see me even when I'm trying not to be seen. And You want to be with me no matter how questionable my reputation!

PRAYER JAR INSPIRATION:

Jesus wants to come to my house today.

FLIPPED

*Do not be conformed to this world, but be transformed by the
renewal of your mind, that by testing you may discern what is
the will of God, what is good and acceptable and perfect.*

ROMANS 12:2 ESV

Do you enjoy watching house-flipping shows on TV? It's remarkable, watching them take a filthy, run-down house and turn it into a thing of beauty. Walls are torn down and rebuilt. New flooring goes in. Paint transforms the rooms into masterpieces.

We love transformational TV because, in an hour, we can watch something morph from ugly to beautiful. (Hey, this is one reason shows about rapid weight loss gained popularity a while back. We just love transformations, whether we're talking about buildings or people!)

God is still in the transformation business. And, while radical transformations don't always happen in rapid fashion like we see on TV, He can transform you from the inside out, no matter how rough your current situation might be.

Like some of those homebuilders, God might have to go to the bare bones and start from scratch with you. He will give you a new foundation in Him and build you into a person of strength and beauty. All you must do is submit to the process and allow Him to do the work.

*There are areas of my life that need to be flipped, Lord.
And I give those areas to You today! Amen.*

PRAYER JAR INSPIRATION:

God is still in the transformation business.

HOW BADLY DO YOU WANT IT?

*Heal me, LORD, and I will be healed; save me and I
will be saved, for you are the one I praise.*

JEREMIAH 17:14 NIV

How badly do you want to be healed? It's a legitimate question. Some people live with their brokenness for so long that they begin to embrace it as a friend.

There are some great stories in the New Testament about people who wanted healing. Badly. First, we discover a story about a woman with an issue of blood. She had struggled for years with this problem, which caused her to be ostracized from society and looked on as unclean. She was so desperate for healing that she decided to work her way through the crowd to touch the hem of Jesus' garment. When she did, she was instantly healed!

Another story of similar desperation is found in Luke 5. The friends of a sick man cut a hole in the roof of a house to drop their sick friend down inside so that Jesus would take notice of him. (It's great to have friends who will believe with you for your healing, isn't it?) Jesus healed that man when He saw the faith of his friends.

These stories raise a legitimate question: How badly do you want it? Today, run straight to Jesus, the one who has healing in His wings.

You're right there, Jesus, just waiting for me to reach out and touch the hem of Your garment! Thank You for being my healer. Amen.

PRAYER JAR INSPIRATION:

I want healing. I really, really want it!

ANOINTED TO BRING GOOD NEWS

*The Spirit of the Lord G*od *is upon me, because the*
*L*ord *anointed me to bring good news to the humble;*
He has sent me to bind up the brokenhearted, to proclaim
release to captives and freedom to prisoners.

Isaiah 61:1 nasb

Healed people heal people. It's true. People who've overcome addiction are better equipped to help those who are currently addicted. A friend who has lost a loved one knows best how to empathize with that friend who has just lost her mother.

The reason it's so important for survivors to be a part of the healing process for the hurting is because they carry a message of hope. They are the good news bearers. And nothing is needed more in a crisis than that one person carrying a banner of hope and positivity.

You can be that person. God has healed you so that you can carry the message of healing to others. No doubt you have friends—fully alive in the Spirit and radiating with hope—who shine their light wherever they go.

You can be like that. You *should* be like that. The world needs more of it.

I want to be a beacon of light, giving this dark world hope.
Give me courage to go forth with radiant positivity, pointing
others to the good news of the gospel, Lord. Amen.

PRAYER JAR INSPIRATION:

I can be a beacon of hope.

FREEDOM

Now the Lord is the Spirit, and where the
Spirit of the Lord is, there is freedom.
2 CORINTHIANS 3:17 ESV

Freedom is a wonderful thing, and it's blissful to walk in it. No matter where you've been, no matter what has held you tightly in its grip, you can be set free. This is the message of the gospel—freedom from sin, freedom from the clutches of hell, and freedom to walk in newness of life.

That old life, the one that had you bound and frightened? It's gone now. When you say yes to Jesus, you become a new you, living in a new era, one filled with possibilities and opportunities. You don't have to go back to the way things used to be.

Shackles have fallen, hope has risen, and there's a sparkle in your eyes now. That's what freedom in Jesus looks like. It doesn't mean you won't still face obstacles (you will), but you can tackle them one by one with your Savior's hand firmly clutched in yours.

So, what's keeping you? There are plenty of good roads ahead for you!

I'm so grateful to walk forward with my hand in Yours, Jesus. Amen.

PRAYER JAR INSPIRATION:

I will walk freedom's road with my head held high!

SCRIPTURE
INDEX

THE OLD TESTAMENT

THE NEW TESTAMENT

IF YOU LOVED *THE PRAYER JAR DEVOTIONAL: HEALING.* . .

You'll also love bestselling author Wanda E. Brunstetter's

THE PRAYER JARS FICTION SERIES

The Hope Jar
978-1-62416-747-8

The Forgiving Jar
978-1-62416-748-5

The Healing Jar
978-1-62416-749-2

Antique jars hidden around an Amish farm are found filled with slips of paper containing thoughts, quotes, and prayers by an unknown author. Three young women each find a jar that takes her on a journey of personal reflection. When the author is revealed, can the jars become a tool to restore a family's lost hopes and faith for the future?